U1019750

汉语口语教程

第四册

北京语言大学出版社
BEIJING LANGUAGE AND CULTURE
UNIVERSITY PRESS

图书在版编目（CIP）数据

汉语口语教程．第四册／杨寄洲，贾永芬编著．——北京 ：北京语言大学出版社，2022.11

ISBN 978-7-5619-6180-3

Ⅰ.①汉… Ⅱ.①杨… ②贾… Ⅲ.①汉语－口语－对外汉语教学－教材 Ⅳ.① H195.4

中国版本图书馆 CIP 数据核字（2022）第 199250 号

汉语口语教程第四册

HANYU KOUYU JIAOCHENG DI-SICE

责任编辑：王巧燕　李金梅
排版制作：北京创艺涵文化发展有限公司
责任印制：周　燚

出版发行：北京语言大学出版社
社　　址：北京市海淀区学院路 15 号，100083
网　　址：www.blcup.com
电子信箱：service@blcup.com
电　　话：编 辑 部　8610-82303647/3592/3724
国内发行　8610-82303650/3591/3648
海外发行　8610-82303365/3080/3668
北语书店　8610-82303653
网购咨询　8610-82303908
印　　刷：北京鑫丰华彩印有限公司

版　　次：2022 年 11 月第 1 版　　印　　次：2022 年 11 月第 1 次印刷
开　　本：787 毫米 × 1092 毫米　1/16　　印　　张：15.5
字　　数：242 千字
定　　价：65.00 元

PRINTED IN CHINA

前言

《汉语口语教程》是为零起点的汉语学习者编写的口语教材，适用于开展学历教育和非学历教育以及各类国际汉语教育的教学单位。

本教程的编写理念是：力求培养学生成才。

选择学习汉语的外国学生，尤其是来华学习汉语的留学生大多处于人生的最佳年龄段，他们万里迢迢来到中国，来到我们身边，追求自己的人生梦想，跟我们学习汉语，我们不能辜负了他们。我们一定要树立培养学生成才的理念，哪怕学生只学一年半载，也要为他们今后的发展着想。

口语课是单项技能训练课。

如果说听力课和阅读课重在输入的话，那么口语课则重在输出。这就要求学生在课堂上要尽可能多地开口说话，要求教师要借助教材，调动和利用一切教学手段和技巧，激发学生的表达欲望。师生之间、生生之间要开展接近实际的交际会话，培养、操练学生的口头表达能力。要让学生通过一年的学习，能够运用汉语满足日常交际需要，并为他们升入高年级或进入其他专业学习（如学医、学工等）打下一个良好的基础。

口语课堂应是师生互动、演示教材的“剧场”。

我们希望，任课教师一定要充分利用课堂，充分利用师生面对面的语境，指导并共同进行师生之间、生生之间的交际会话。课堂交际会话当然是模拟实际生活的会话，尽管如此，这四五十分钟的一节课，对于学生来说都弥足珍贵。我们建议教师不要过多地使用PPT，您面对学生真诚坦然的微笑，亲切悦耳的话语，声情并茂的讲解与朗读，与学生面对面、心与心的交流，这是任何教材、任何课件都无法代替的。

口语课堂上，教师和学生都要动起来。再好的教材都是死的。语言是交际的工具，是最灵动、最活泼、最实用的。尤其是初级阶段，学生能不能尽快用汉语进行最实用的交际，对他们影响巨大而深远。

口语应是带表情的动与说的结合。所以建议教师活用教材，把课堂当成“剧场”，把教材当成“剧本”，教师当好导演，学生当好演员，师生互动，把每节课都演成一幕话剧。

本教程分4册共64课，供零起点的汉语学习者使用1年。4册书共出生词约2000个，多为常用词。

鉴于各个教学单位口语课的课时不统一，有多有少。所以，完全可以从本单位的实际出发，从教学对象的实际出发，灵活使用本教程。

编写体例

一、课文

本教程的课文多是情景会话。情景设计都基于来华留学生的学习和生活。编者的意图是，学习和练习这些会话，使学习者能熟练地运用它们，满足日常学习和生活的交际需要。

为了尽早培养学生的成段表达能力，本教程从第一册第10课起，就设置了一个“读后说”的练习项目。其内容都是一些小短文。

课文是重中之重！

课堂上教师要集中精力，用大量时间带领学生把课文读熟。教师要大声示范朗读，大声领读；同时，要求学生大声跟读、大声齐读、大声地单独朗读。

朗读是口语课堂教学和课外练习的主要方法。要鼓励学生大声地、反复地朗读，让学生通过朗读感受汉语的语音语调和语气，领略汉语的语言美。不论是会话课文还是叙述短文，都要求学生最少要朗读十遍以上，达到熟读成诵的程度。这样，也只有这样，用的时候才能脱口而出。

通过一年的训练，大多数学生的口语能力应能基本满足日常学习和生活的交际需要。这是被多年教学实践证明了的。

第一、二册（1～32课）的课文都配有汉语拼音，同时提供英文译文供学生参考。拼音是为了减少学生朗读的困难，英文译文是为了减少学生理解的困难。我们的教学对象大多具有高中以上学历，尽管英语不一定是每个学生的母语，但本教程的内容都是基础的日常会话，英文译文对他们理解课文应该有所帮助。

第三、四册（33～64课）除了生词加注拼音和英文释义外，课文不再加注拼音，也不再提供英文译文。

效果如何，要由教学实践来检验。我们希望听到一线教师的意见和建议，以便及时修正。

二、生词

本教程每课的生词部分都有拼音和英文释义。

三、注释

口语课堂教学没有讲练语法的任务，因此，本教程的注释只是对课文中出现的一些语法点或重点词语的用法加以简要的说明，为教师教学提供一些方便。例句可供学习者参考。

四、练习

口语课重在培养学生“说”的言语技能，但听说读写这四项言语技能既相对独立又相互依存，既相互制约又相互促进。听不懂，一定不会说；读不懂，也一定影响说。没有大量的输入，不可能有理想的输出。因此，口语课要达到预期的效果，必须充分利用各项言语技能的相互促进作用，通过有效的输入，激发表达欲望，促进齿舌运动，使学习者发出正确的汉语语音语调，说出正确的有交际意义的句子，从而达到日常学习和生活想要达到的交际目的。

本教程通用的练习是：朗读并分辨近音字词的语音语调、替换、选词填空、完成句子或会话并大声朗读、结合自身实际回答问题等。

口语课必须重视语音语调的训练。因此，本教程始终把语音语调的练习放在非常重要的位置。教材在这方面的努力，也是为教学做个提示：要想让学生说一口正确的汉语普通话，教师的作用是教材无法代替的。

练习要求学生课外完成，教师可及时检查和纠正，以提高学生的学习质量。

练习不仅是复练课堂所学，同时希望学生能够通过做练习，培养自学能力。严格地说，没有自学能力的学生不可能成才。在网络时代，只要想学、爱学，随时都可以学习。要引导学生刻苦自学、努力成才。所以，本教程在练习中一再提示，遇到不懂的词语、不懂的文化知识点，要去问百度、问谷歌，要随手去查电子词典——它们都是课外的“老师”。教师要鼓励学生自学，帮助学生培养良好的学习习惯。

在初级阶段，受词汇、语法的制约，会话课文都是情景会话。情景会话就必然受情景的限定。为了弥补初级口语会话的不足，我们在每课练习部分的最后，添加了一个“怎么表达”，这实际就是交际会话。一般说来，交际会话的句子和会话不太受情景的制约。需要说明的是，这也不属于课堂教学的内容，而是为学生自学准备的。

练习中的诗词和著名词句都是学生自学的内容。出诗词的目的是想利用其合辙押韵的特点，培养学生的朗读兴趣，同时也为他们今后的深造奠定基础。一些我们耳熟能详的词句，让学生接触一下，不无益处。

本教程的编写得到业内朋友的指导和帮助，北京语言大学出版社也给予大力支持，在此表示衷心的感谢。

编者

2022 年 6 月

Preface

Spoken Chinese Course is written for Chinese beginners. It is suitable for the academic institutions developing credential and non-credential education, as well as teaching Chinese to speakers of other languages.

The compiling idea of this course is to strive to cultivate students' talents.

The foreign students who choose to study Chinese, especially those who come to China to study Chinese, are at their best ages in life. They come all the way to China, to us, to pursue their dreams of life and learn Chinese with us, thus we can't let them down. We must hold the belief to cultivate students' talents. Even if they just study for a year or so, we should consider their future development.

The oral class is a single-skill training course.

While the listening and reading classes focus on input, the oral class stresses output. Therefore, students are required to speak as much as possible in class, and teachers are required to stimulate students' desire to express themselves adopting all kinds of teaching methods and techniques by the aid of the coursebook. Genuine conversations should take place between the teacher and students, as well as among students, in order to develop and train students' oral expression ability. After one year's study, students should be able to have daily communication in Chinese, and lay a solid foundation for their further study in higher grades or other majors (e.g. medicine, engineering, etc.).

The oral class should be a theater for the teacher to interact with students and demonstrate the coursebook.

We hope that the teacher can make full use of the class and the face-to-face context between him/her and students to guide and make teacher-student and student-student conversations. Classroom conversation is of course a conversation that stimulates real life. Nevertheless, the 40- to 50-minute lesson is especially valuable for students. We suggest teachers try not to use PPT too much. Your sincere and calm smile, kind and sweet words, remarkable explanation and reading aloud, and your face-to-face and heart-to-heart communication with students cannot be replaced by any coursebook or courseware.

In the oral class, both the teacher and students should be active. No matter how good the coursebook is, it is rigid. Language is the tool of communication. It is the most intelligent, active and practical. Especially in the primary stage, whether students can use Chinese to communicate as soon as possible has a huge and far-reaching impact on them.

Spoken language should be a combination of expressive movement and speech. So teachers are advised to make flexible use of the coursebook. Teachers should take the classroom as a theater and the coursebook as the playscript. The teacher should act as the director, while students should act as actors and actresses. They should interact with each other to put on a play in each class.

This course contains four books with 64 lessons. It is suitable for Chinese beginners and can be used for one year. There are about 2,000 new words in the four books, most of which are common words.

Since the hours for the oral class vary in each institution, you can use this coursebook flexibly according to the actual conditions of your institution and your students.

Compiling style:

I. Texts

The texts in this coursebook are mostly situation conversations. The situations are based on the study and life of foreign students in China. The compilers aim to make students learn and practice these conversations so as to use them proficiently and meet their communicative needs in study and life.

In order to develop students' ability to express themselves in paragraph as early as possible, a "speaking after reading" part is designed from Lesson 10 of Book 1. All the texts in this part are short essays.

Texts are the most important!

In class, the teacher should focus on texts and spend much time to lead students to read texts fluently. The teacher should model reading aloud and ask students to follow, and read aloud together and individually.

Reading aloud is the main method of oral classroom teaching and extracurricular practice. Encourage students to read aloud and repeatedly. Let students perceive the pronunciation, intonation and tones of Chinese and the beauty of Chinese by reading aloud.

Whether it is a conversation text or a narrative essay, the teacher should require students to read it aloud for at least ten times to reach the level of reciting it. In this way, and only in this way, can students blurt it out when using it.

Through one year's training, most students should be able to communicate in their daily study and life. This has been proved by years of teaching practice.

Pinyin and English translation for the texts are provided in Books 1 and 2 (Lessons 1-32). The Pinyin is added to make it easier for students to read the texts aloud, and the English translation is provided to reduce students' difficulty in understanding. Most of our students have a senior high school education or above. Although English is not necessarily every student's first language, all the content of this coursebook is basic and daily conversations, and the English translation should be helpful for them to understand the texts.

In Books 3 and 4 (Lessons 33-64), except for the Pinyin and English definition for the new words, no Pinyin and English translation for the texts are provided. The effect will be tested by the teaching practice. We hope to hear the opinions and suggestions from the teachers, so as to make timely revisions.

II. New Words

The Pinyin and English definition are provided for the new words in each lesson in the coursebook.

III. Notes

Grammar is not taught and practiced in the oral class. Therefore, the notes in this coursebook are only brief explanations of some grammatical points or key words and expressions that appear in the texts, to provide convenience for teaching. Example sentences are for students' reference.

IV. Exercises

Oral class focuses on developing students' speaking skills. However, the four language skills of listening, speaking, reading and writing are relatively independent on one hand, but dependent on each other on the other hand. If you don't understand what was said, you can't speak. If you don't understand what was written, your speaking skills will also be affected. Without a large amount of input, it is impossible to have ideal output. Therefore, to achieve the expected effect in oral class, we must make full use of the mutual promotion of various language skills. Through effective input, the desire to express is stimulated, and the tongue and teeth movements are promoted. Students are able to produce correct pronunciation and intonation of Chinese, and say the correct sentences with communicative meanings, so as to achieve the communicative purpose needed in daily study and life.

The common exercises in this coursebook include reading aloud and distinguishing the pronunciation and intonation of similar words, substitution, choosing words to fill in the blanks, completing the sentences or conversations and reading them aloud, and answering the questions according to the students' actual situations.

The training of pronunciation and intonation is very important in oral class. Therefore, this coursebook always attaches great importance to the pronunciation and intonation exercises. The effort of the coursebook in this regard is also a reminder for teaching: to make students speak Mandarin correctly, the role of teachers cannot be replaced by coursebooks.

Students are required to finish the exercises after class. Teachers can check and correct them in time to improve the quality of students' study.

The exercises are designed not only to practice what students have learned in class, but also to train students' self-study ability. Strictly speaking, students without self-study ability can't be successful. In the Internet age, as long as you want to and love to learn, you can learn at any time. Teachers should guide students to study hard independently and become successful. Therefore, the course in the exercises always suggests students to consult Baidu, Google, or electronic dictionaries when meeting unfamiliar words, expressions or cultural knowledge, for they are extracurricular "teachers". Teachers should encourage students to study by themselves and help them develop good study habits.

Restricted by vocabulary and grammar in the primary stage, all the conversational texts are situation conversations. In order to make up for the deficiency of primary oral conversations, we add a "how to express" part at the end of the exercises in each lesson. They are actually communicative conversations. Generally speaking, communicative sentences and conversations are less situational. It should be noted that this part is prepared for students to study on their own instead of being taught in class.

The well-known sayings in the exercises are for students to study on their own. The purpose is to guide students to perceive the rhymes in the poems so as to develop their interests in reading aloud and lay a foundation for their further study. It is useful for students to get an initial understanding of some poems and sentences we are familiar with.

We sincerely appreciate the guidance and help from friends in this field, as well as the strong support by Beijing Language and Culture University Press when compiling this coursebook.

The Author

June 2022

致学习者

亲爱的同学们：

当你拿起这本书，开始学习汉语口语的时候，你的人生便开始了新的旅程。

当你离开家乡，告别父母、兄弟、同学、朋友来到中国这个陌生国度的时候，你可能有诸多的不适应。

不过没关系。任何人初到异国他乡，都会有这种感觉的。

初来乍到，一句汉语也不会说，一个汉字也不认识，一个朋友都没有，你会感到孤单、寂寞，你会感到无助、痛苦。想家，想爸爸妈妈，想兄弟姐妹，想同学朋友，甚至会哭鼻子，恨不得马上飞回国去。

不过，你一定明白，眼前的这些困难都是暂时的，很快就会过去；过去了，你将由此踏上成才之路。

你要想到自己的未来，想到你是在学习人类最美的语言之一，也是当今世界历史最悠久、使用人数最多的语言之一——汉语！

汉语之美，美不胜收；汉字之妙，妙不可言。

要让自己冷静下来，想一想：今后的路该怎么走？

不必讳言，对于来自世界各国的学习者来说，汉语的确很难学。尽管书里说不难，但是老师心里明白，学好一种外语，对谁来说都不容易。

但“艰难困苦，玉汝于成”，“吃得苦中苦，才有甜上甜”。不经历风雨，难以见彩虹，没有人能随随便便地成功。希望你放平心态，放松心情，准备迎接各种挑战。为了你，为了你的家人，相信你一定不怕苦、不怕难，勇敢地闯过一道道难关，胜利到达成功的彼岸，实现自己美好的理想，成就自己理想的人生。

为此，根据我们几十年教外国留学生的经验，向同学们提出以下几点希望。

1. 无论如何，都应该坚持每天到教室上课

学得好的学生不一定是班上最聪明的学生，但一定是最努力的学生。希望同学们能天天和你的老师、同学见面，天天和他们一起度过这愉快美好的课堂时光。上课不仅仅是学汉语，更是为了培养自己高尚的人品和高贵的人格，使自己成为一个自律且优秀的人。

2．课后一定要认真做练习

学习外语，遇到不会、不懂的词语和句子是难免的。如今是网络时代，只要你想学，处处都能找到老师。所以我们一再强调：问百度、问谷歌、查电子词典。

要努力培养自己的自学能力。可以说，没有自学能力的人不可能成才。世界上凡是学有所成的人，都有非凡的自学能力。

老师领进门，修行在个人。

那些杰出的、优秀的人虽然都有老师，但他们最后都比自己的老师更优秀！也希望你们能踏着老师的肩膀，奋勇地攀登你们人生的高峰。

3. 要预习，预习比复习更重要

要变“要我学”为“我要学”，使自己时时处于主动的地位。

我们说预习比复习更重要，就是因为预习是你在主动地学。

学习外语，一定要走在老师的前边。现在的学习条件这么好，只要你有志气、肯努力，就要在上课前，把第二天要学的课文、生词都预习预习，一遍、两遍……，或者读一读、记一记。这样，你到教室去上课，将不会再有“难”的苦恼，而会觉得是一种美妙的享受。

4. 多和中国人交往

语言是交际的工具。到生活中去，到中国社会中去，社会生活永远有课堂上学不到的东西。要相信，人类的大多数都是善良的，中国人也一样。只要你不怕、不害羞，你就会明白，在家靠父母，出门靠朋友。多交朋友，一定是一件非常惬意的事。在中国人面前说汉语，不要怕说错。要多说，一次说错了，再说一次可能就说对了。要不了多久，你一定能说一口流利的汉语，你的生活也会开辟一片新的天地。

至于将来做什么，将来会怎么样，请你多读书，书会告诉你的。

这本书和教这本书的老师都是你的朋友，他们将陪伴你一路走去，走向你理想的未来。

最想说的是：我们爱你们，所以献上这本书！

编者

2021 年 6 月初稿

2022 年 6 月定稿

To Students

Dear students,

When you pick up this book and begin to learn spoken Chinese, your will start a new journey in your life.

When you leave your hometown, say goodbye to your parents, siblings, classmates and friends, and come to China—an unfamiliar country, you may feel much unadapted.

But it doesn't matter. Any new arrival to an alien place will have the same feeling.

When you first arrive in China, you cannot speak a word of Chinese, nor can you recognize any Chinese characters, or have any friends. You feel lonely, helpless and miserable. You miss your parents, siblings, classmates and friends. You even want to cry. You wish you would fly home immediately.

However, you must know that these immediate difficulties are temporary and will soon be overcome. When you overcome them, you will be on the road to success.

You have to think about your future, and that you are studying one of the most beautiful human languages, as well as one of the oldest and most spoken languages in the world today—Chinese!

The beauty of Chinese is too much to absorb. The wonder of Chinese characters is beyond expression.

You should calm yourself down and think about your road in future.

There is no denying the fact that Chinese is really difficult for students from all over the world. Although it is said in the books that Chinese is not difficult, teachers know that studying a foreign language well is not easy for anyone.

However, no pains, no gains. We hope that you will be prepared for challenges in a peaceful state of mind. For you and your family, we believe you won't be afraid of the difficulties and hardships, and you will get over the hurdles bravely before reaching the dreamland of success, realizing your goals, and achieving your ideal life.

To this end, based on our decades of experience in teaching foreign students, we hope you can do as follows:

1. Persist in attending class every day in any case

Those who do well in class are not necessarily the smartest students, but surely the most hard-working ones. We hope you can meet your teachers and classmates every day and spend the happy time with them in class. By attending class, you not only learn Chinese, but also cultivate noble character and make yourself a self-disciplined and excellent person.

2. Do exercises carefully after class

When studying a foreign language, it is inevitable to encounter words and sentences that you don't know or understand. In the Internet age, teachers can be found everywhere if you want to learn something. That's why we emphasize again and again that you should consult Baidu, Google, and electronic dictionaries.

Efforts should be made to develop your self-study ability. A person without the self-study ability cannot be successful. Anyone in the world who is successful in learning has an extraordinary self-study ability.

The teacher may teach, but progress is up to the hard work of the individual.

Though those outstanding people have teachers, they become more excellent than their teachers in the end! We also hope that you can also stand on the shoulders of your teachers and climb the peak of your life bravely.

3. Pay attention to previewing, which is more important than reviewing

Change "make me study" to "I want to study", and take the initiative all the time. Previewing is more important than reviewing in that you are studying on your own initiative when you preview.

When you learn a foreign language, be sure to stay ahead of your teachers. Now the learning conditions are good. As long as you are ambitious and hard-working, you can preview, read and memorize the text and new words several times before class. In this way, when you go to class, you will feel wonderful rather than difficult.

4. Make more contact with Chinese people

Language is a tool of communication. You should experience Chinese life and society, where you can learn what you cannot learn in class. People are mostly kind, so are Chinese. As long as you are not afraid or shy, you will find that you need the support of friends when away from home. It is very pleasant to make more friends. Don't be afraid of making mistakes when speaking Chinese in front of Chinese people. Talk more. If you make a mistake at first, try again and you will probably be right. You will shortly be able to speak Chinese fluently. In addition, you will explore a new world in your life.

As to your future, read more books and you will find the answer.

Both this coursebook and the teacher who uses it in class are your friends, who will accompany you all the way to your ideal future.

What we want to say most is that we offer this book because we love you!

The Author

First draft in June 2021

Final version in February 2022

一、汉语词类简称表

名称	简称	英文
1. 名词 míngcí	名	noun
2. 代词 dàicí	代	pronoun
3. 动词 dòngcí	动	verb
4. 助动词 zhùdòngcí	助动	auxiliary verb
5. 形容词 xíngróngcí	形	adjective
6. 数词 shùcí	数	numeral
7. 量词 liàngcí	量	measure word
8. 副词 fùcí	副	adverb
9. 介词 jiècí	介	preposition
10. 连词 liáncí	连	conjunction
11. 叹词 tàncí	叹	interjection
12. 拟声词 nǐshēngcí	拟声	onomatopoeia
13. 助词 zhùcí	助	particle
14. 词头 cítóu	头	prefix
15. 词尾 cíwěi	尾	suffix

二、汉语语法术语

1. 主语 zhǔyǔ　subject
2. 谓语 wèiyǔ　predicate
3. 宾语 bīnyǔ　object
4. 定语 dìngyǔ　attribute
5. 状语 zhuàngyǔ　adverbial
6. 补语 bǔyǔ　complement

（1）程度补语 chéngdù bǔyǔ　degree complement

例如：形容词＋极了

这个电影好<u>极了</u>。

（2）状态补语 zhuàngtài bǔyǔ　　state complement

例如：动词＋得＋形容词 / 动词短语

他学得好不好？他学得很好。

他跑得快不快？他跑得不快。

你写得怎么样？我写得不太好。

他高兴得跳了起来。

（3）结果补语 jiéguǒ bǔyǔ　　result complement

例如：动词＋动词 / 形容词

我的作业做完了。

瓶子里的酒喝光了。

他把这本书翻译成了英语。

（4）趋向补语 qūxiàng bǔyǔ　　complement of direction

例如：动词＋来 / 去 / 上 / 下 / 进 / 出 / 回 / 过 / 起 / 上来 / 下去 / 回来 / 回去 / 过来 / 过去 / 起来 / 进来 / 进去……

他从楼上下来了。

我们从这儿上去吧。

我买回来一盆花。

他从外边里带进来一只小狗。

（5）可能补语 kěnéng bǔyǔ　　complement of potentiality

例如：动词＋得 / 不＋结果补语 / 趋向补语

中文报你看得懂看不懂？

我现在还听不懂中文广播。

屋子太小，坐不下二十个人。

你买得太多了，我吃不了。

沙发太大，搬不进去。

太重了，我提不动。

（6）数量补语 shùliàng bǔyǔ　　complement of quantity

例如：动词＋数量短语

他比我高五厘米。

姐姐比我大两岁。

（7）时量补语 shíliàng bǔyǔ　　complement of duration

例如：动词＋时量短语

我已经学了一年了。

他来了快一个月了。

（8）动量补语 dòngliàng bǔyǔ　　complement of frequency

例如：动词＋动量短语

我敲了一下门，但是没有人答应。

中国我已经来过两次了。

我把这篇文章从头到尾仔细看了一遍，没有发现错字。

香港我去过一回，台湾我还没有去过。

目录 Contents

Dì-sìshíjiǔ kè Zhòng zài cānyù

第四十九课 重在参与

Lesson 49 Participation is more important than anything else

一 课文 Text

（一）重在参与

大卫：大学运动会就要到了，你报名了吗？

吉米：我报了。

大卫：你参加什么项目？

吉米：我准备参加的是一百米赛跑。你呢？

大卫：我也报名了，我参加四百米跨栏。

吉米：你觉得有希望夺冠吗？

大卫：能不能夺冠无所谓，重在参与嘛。

吉米：我也是这样想的，参赛是为了追求高尚的体育精神！

（二）兰笛，加油！

（运动场上）

裁判：各就各位，预备——（啪！）

A：兰笛，加油！

B：这位姑娘是谁呀？她跑得真快。

A：她是我们班的兰笛，她以前得过百米赛冠军呢！

B：她现在遥遥领先。

A：好！兰笛第一个跑到了终点。她得了第一名！真棒！我们班的兰笛在女子百米赛中跑了个第一。（喊）兰笛，祝贺你！

（三）他也是冠军

A：下面是四百米跨栏，开始了，快看！

B：啊，糟糕！大卫被栏杆绊倒了。真遗憾，四百米跨栏赛他本来能夺冠的。

A：你看，他又爬起来了，又跑过来了。

B：啊！他受伤了，他跨过了一个栏杆，又跨过一个，又一个，大卫，加油！

（大家：加油！加油！）

A：你听！大家都在为他加油呢！

B：他坚持跑到了终点，真是好样儿的！啊，我都要流泪了。

A：体育比赛，不只是为了夺冠，更是为了健身，为了追求这种高尚的精神。所以，今天他也是冠军，也是英雄！

B：对！你说得太对了！

二 生词 New Words

1	重	zhòng	形	important
2	参与	cānyù	动	participate in; take part in
3	运动会	yùndònghuì	名	sports meeting
4	报名	bào míng	动	apply; sign up
5	项目	xiàngmù	名	sports event
6	赛跑	sàipǎo	动	(running) race
7	跨	kuà	动	stride
8	栏（杆）	lán (gān)	名	hurdle
9	夺冠	duó guàn	动	win the championship
10	参赛	cānsài	动	take part in a match
11	高尚	gāoshàng	形	noble

12 体育	tǐyù	名	sports
13 精神	jīngshén	名	spirit
14 裁判	cáipàn	名、动	referee; judge
15 各就各位	gèjiù-gèwèi		on your marks
各	gè	代、副	each; apiece
16 预备	yùbèi	动	get ready
17 啪	pā	拟声	*indicating the sound of clapping, striking, or shooting*
18 加油	jiā yóu	动	come on
19 遥遥领先	yáoyáo-lǐngxiān		be far ahead; hold a safe lead
20 终点	zhōngdiǎn	名	finishing line
21 喊	hǎn	动	call; yell; shout
22 祝贺	zhùhè	动	congratulate
23 绊	bàn	动	(cause to) stumble
24 倒	dǎo	动	fall; tumble down
25 遗憾	yíhàn	形、名	regretful; regret
26 本来	běnlái	副、形	originally; original
27 受伤	shòu shāng	动	be injured; be wounded
28 好样儿的	hǎoyàngrde	名	great fellow
29 流泪	liúlèi	动	shed tears
流	liú	动	shed (tears)
泪	lèi	名	tear; teardrop
30 英雄	yīngxióng	名	hero

专名 Zhuānmíng Proper Noun

大卫	Dàwèi	name of a person

三 注释 Notes

（一）重在参与

“重在参与”表示重要的是参加，言外之意是，别的都不重要。

“重在参与”means it is important to participate, implicating that nothing else matters.

（二）本来

副词“本来”有原先、先前和理所当然的意思，在句子中做状语。例如：

The adverb“本来”means at first, formerly or deservedly. It is usually used as an adverb in a sentence. For example:

1. 我<u>本来</u>不想参加，但后来看朋友参加了，我就也参加了。
2. 真遗憾，四百米跨栏赛他<u>本来</u>能赢的。
3. 你是学生，<u>本来</u>就应该天天去上课。

四 练习 Exercises

（一）朗读 Read aloud

1. 朗读下列发音相近的词语 Read aloud the following words with similar pronunciation

cānjiā 参加	chān jiǎ 掺 假	duó guàn 夺 冠	duō guǎn 多 管
cānyù 参与	cānyǐ 餐椅	yùbèi 预备	yí bèi 一倍
zāogāo 糟糕	zǎogāo 枣糕	yīngxióng 英雄	yīngyǒng 英勇

2. 朗读下列短语 Read the following phrases aloud

准备：准备参加　准备考试　准备得很好　没有准备

得：得冠军　得亚军　得第一　得到了　没得到

祝贺：祝贺你　祝贺生日　表示祝贺　热烈祝贺
糟糕：真糟糕　非常糟糕　糟糕得很　考得很糟糕
遗憾：很遗憾　非常遗憾　表示遗憾　遗憾得很
本来：本来能赢　本来不想参加　本来没报名　本来不愿意

3. 朗读下列被动句，然后再用“把”字句说出以下句子 Read the following passive sentences aloud, then remake these sentences with the “把” sentence

例如：他被栏杆绊倒了。→ 栏杆把他绊倒了。

（1）刚买的手机就被我摔坏了。→

________________________________。

（2）大门口的树被风刮倒了。→

________________________________。

（3）我的背包叫朋友借走了。→

________________________________。

（4）我刚睡着，就被手机铃声吵醒了。→

________________________________。

（5）我的车让同学骑去了。→

________________________________。

（6）那棵小树被大风刮倒了。→

________________________________。

（二）**替换并朗读** Replace and read aloud

1. A：你参加什么项目？
   B：我参加的是<u>一百米赛跑</u>。

四百米跨栏	篮球比赛
游泳	跳高
跳远	自行车比赛

2. A：有希望<u>夺</u> <u>冠</u>吗？
   B：<u>夺</u>不<u>夺</u> <u>冠</u>无所谓。

得　奖	拿　奖学金
选　上	得　第一

3. 她跑得真快。

跳	高	跳	远
来	早	写	好
画	美	打扮	漂亮

4. 糟糕！他被栏杆绊倒了。

她	自行车	撞上
课本	雨	淋湿
我	雪	滑倒
手机	我	摔坏
他	足球	砸（zá, pound）到
他	感冒	传染（chuánrǎn, infect）上

（三）选词填空并朗读下列句子 Choose the appropriate words to fill in the blanks and read aloud the following sentences

在　呢　了　精神　米　有

1. 大学运动会就要到________，你报名了吗？
2. 我准备参加的是一百米赛跑。你________？
3. 我也报名了，我参加四百________跨栏。
4. 你觉得________希望夺冠吗？
5. 能不能夺冠无所谓，重________参与嘛。
6. 我也是这样想的，参赛是为了追求高尚的体育________！

无所谓　保持　糟糕　本来　准备　祝贺　重在　遗憾

1. 遇到困难的时候，不要怕！________坚持，坚持就可能成功。
2. 体育比赛的冠军只有一个，以夺不夺冠________的心态参加比赛，才能真正享受比赛。
3. 我________一年后去医科大学学中医。

4. 能加上你的微信吗？我希望跟你________联系。

5. 真________，刚买的手机就被我摔坏了。

6. ________你得到这个大学的奖学金。

7. 昨晚的比赛非常精彩，你没有看就太________了！

8. 我________也住留学生公寓，后来为了提高汉语口语水平，才到一个中国人家去住的。

（四）你是 A，请你向 B 提问 Supposing you are A, ask B questions

1. A：____?
   B：我报名参加了。

2. A：____?
   B：我一百米的记录是十五秒。

3. A：____?
   B：对我来说，得不得第一名无所谓。

4. A：____?
   B：我每天都坚持锻炼一个小时。

5. A：____?
   B：我对这个成绩很满意。

6. A：____?
   B：参加体育运动的目的是健身，不是夺得冠军。

（五）和同学一起表演课文 Act out the text with your classmates

（六）自由表达 Express yourself freely

看电视台的一个体育比赛节目，边看边用汉语介绍，看自己能说多少。

（七）读后说 Read the passage and say it

1. 朗读 Read aloud

学，永远不晚

日语学习班开学报名那天，来了一位老人。

“给孩子报名？”负责报名的工作人员问。

“不，给我自己。”老人回答。

工作人员觉得很奇怪，屋里那些年轻的报名者也有点儿吃惊，有人还笑了。

老人解释说：“儿子在日本找了爱人，他们每次回来，说话叽里咕噜，我听得着急，我想听懂他们说的话。”

“大爷，您多大年纪了？”工作人员问。

“六十八了。”

“您要想听懂他们说的话，最少得学两年。可两年以后，您都七十岁了。”

老人笑着反问：“姑娘，你以为我不学，两年以后就是六十六吗？”

听了老人的话，大家肃然起敬。工作人员也很快给老人办了报名手续。

是呀，老人学与不学，两年以后都是七十岁。不同的是：学了能开心地跟儿媳妇用日语交谈，不学则仍然像木偶一样在旁边待着。

小词典

负责	fùzé	动、形	be responsible for; be in charge of; responsible
奇怪	qíguài	形	strange
吃惊	chī jīng	动	surprise
解释	jiěshì	动	explain
叽里咕噜	jīligūlū	拟声	talk indistinctly or inaudibly about
反问	fǎnwèn	动	ask (a question) in reply
肃然起敬	sùrán-qǐjìng		be filled with deep veneration
手续	shǒuxù	名	procedure
开心	kāixīn	形、动	happy; feel happy
仍然	réngrán	副	still; as before
木偶	mù'ǒu	名	puppet

2. 朗读下列问句并回答 Read aloud the following interrogative sentences and answer them

（1）老人来日语学习班做什么？

（2）老人多大年纪了？

（3）老人为什么要学习日语？

（4）负责报名的工作人员为什么感到奇怪？

（5）老人怎么反问这位工作人员的？

（6）学与不学对老人来说，有什么不同？

3. 你是 A，请你向 B 提问 Supposing you are A, ask B questions

（1）A：________________________________?

（什么　人）

B：日语学习班开学报名时，来了一位老人。

（2）A：________________________________?

（谁　报名）

B：负责报名的工作人员以为老人是给孩子报名的。

（3）A：________________________________?

（什么　反应）

B：听说老人给自己报名时，工作人员感到很奇怪。屋里那些年轻的报名者也有点儿吃惊，有人还笑了。

（4）A：________________________________?

（为什么）

B：老人解释说，他儿子在日本找了个爱人，他们每次回来，说话叽里咕噜，老人听得着急。为了能听懂他们说的话，所以他才想学日语。

（5）A：________________________________?

（多大　年纪）

B：六十八了。

（6）A：________________________________？

（以后　什么　反应）

B：听了老人的话，大家肃然起敬。工作人员也很快给老人办了报名手续。

（八）朗读中国经典诗词，请注意语音语调 Read aloud the classic Chinese poem and pay attention to the pronunciation and intonation

Wàng Yuè
望岳

[Táng] Dù Fǔ
［唐］杜甫（712—770）

Dàizōng fú rúhé? Qí-Lǔ qīng wèi liǎo.
岱宗夫如何？齐鲁青未了。
Zàohuà zhōng shén xiù, yīnyáng gē hūn xiǎo.
造化钟神秀，阴阳割昏晓。
Dàng xiōng shēng céng yún, jué zì rù guī niǎo.
荡胸生层云，决眦入归鸟。
Huì dāng líng juédǐng, yìlǎn zhòng shān xiǎo.
会当凌绝顶，一览众山小。

（九）请欣赏下列著名的词句 Please enjoy the following famous saying

Mǎn zhāo sǔn, qiān shòu yì.
满招损，谦受益。

Pride hurts, modesty benefits.

Dì-wǔshí kè　　Zhēnjiǔ zhēn líng

第五十课　针灸真灵

Lesson 50　Acupuncture is really effective

一　课文 Text

（一）是大夫用针灸给我治好的

爱德华：你的腰还疼吗？

常　浩：早好了。

爱德华：怎么好的？

常　浩：针灸，是大夫用针灸给我治好的。

爱德华：针灸有那么灵吗？

常　浩：不信你也试试。你看，我的腰以前总疼，现在完全好了。

爱德华：最近，我的腿有点儿疼，我也想去让大夫给我扎扎针。

（二）按摩以后你就知道了

大夫：你怎么了？

戴维：今天早上一起床，脖子就疼得厉害。

大夫：是落枕了。来，你坐下来，我给你按摩按摩。

戴维：按摩？怎么按摩？

大夫：我按摩以后你就知道了。

（按摩以后）

大夫：好，你再抬抬头，动动脖子，看还疼不疼了？

戴维：哎，好多了，真的不怎么疼了，好神奇呀！谢谢大夫！

（三）我早听说过中医很神奇

玛丽：戴维，你的脖子好了吗？还疼不疼了？

戴维：谢谢你的关心，已经好了，现在一点儿也不疼了。

玛丽：你吃的什么药？

戴维：我什么药也没吃。

玛丽：什么药都没吃？那是怎么好的？

戴维：是大夫给我按摩按好的。

玛丽：是吗？按摩有那么灵吗？

戴维：按摩真的很灵。开始我也不相信，大夫按摩了以后马上就觉得不怎么疼了，我这才相信的。按摩真好，又舒服又治病。

玛丽：其实，我早就听说过中医很神奇，针灸和按摩能治病。但是一直搞不明白针灸和按摩是什么原理。

戴维：你看，这是我前几天买的一本书。书上是这么说的，我给你念念：中医认为人的身体是一个由经络和穴位组成的世界，经络和穴位遍布全身。中医用针灸或按摩刺激这些穴位，疏通经络，来维持身体各个器官正常的生理功能，从而达到治疗各种疾病的目的。

玛丽：啊，这么复杂，简直不可思议。

二 生词 New Words

1	针灸	zhēnjiǔ	名	acupuncture
	针	zhēn	名	needle
2	腰	yāo	名	waist
3	完全	wánquán	副、形	completely; fully; absolute
4	最近	zuìjìn	名	recently

5 脖子	bózi	名	neck
6 落枕	lào zhěn	动	have a stiff neck (caused by cold or awkward sleeping posture)
7 抬	tái	动	lift; raise
8 哎	āi	叹	*expressing surprise or dissatisfaction*
9 相信	xiāngxìn	动	believe
10 其实	qíshí	副	in fact; as a matter of fact; actually
11 神奇	shénqí	形	magical; mystical; miraculous
12 原理	yuánlǐ	名	principle; theory
13 念	niàn	动	read
14 认为	rènwéi	动	think; believe
15 由	yóu	介	(*used for showing how or in what way sth. is done*) by
16 经络	jīngluò	名	main and collateral channel
17 穴位	xuéwèi	名	acupuncture point; acupoint
18 组成	zǔchéng	动	form; make up; compose
19 遍布	biànbù	动	be found everywhere; spread all over
20 全身	quánshēn	名	all over (the body); from head to foot
21 刺激	cìjī	动	stimulate
22 疏通	shūtōng	动	dredge
23 维持	wéichí	动	maintain; keep
24 器官	qìguān	名	organ
25 生理	shēnglǐ	名	physiology
26 从而	cóng'ér	连	thus; thereby; hence
27 达到	dá dào	动	achieve; attain; reach

28 治疗	zhìliáo	动	(by means of medicine, operation, etc.) treat; cure
29 疾病	jíbìng	名	disease; illness
30 复杂	fùzá	形	complicated; complex
31 不可思议	bùkě-sīyì		inconceivable; unimaginable

专名 Zhuānmíng Proper Noun

戴维	Dàiwéi	name of a person

三 注释 Notes

(一) 其实

副词"其实"表示所说的情况是真实的，用在动词或主语前。在句子中引出和上文相反的意思，有更正上文的作用，或对上文所说加以补充。例如：

The adverb "其实" means that what is said is true. It is usually put before a verb or subject. In a sentence, it is used to introduce the meaning opposite to what is previously said and to correct or make additional explanation to what was said above. For example:

1. 其实，我早听说过中医很神奇，针灸和按摩能治病。
2. 你说他回国了，其实他没有回国，而是到南方旅行去了。
3. 你看他像老师，其实他是学生。

(二) 认为

动词"认为"表示对人或事物有某种看法，做出某种判断，在句中做谓语。例如：

The verb "认为" means to have a certain opinion on somebody or something, and to make some judgment. It is used as a predicate in a sentence. For example:

1. 中医认为人的身体是一个由经络和穴位组成的世界。

2. 他认为中医中药是中国文化的重要组成部分。
3. 我认为每个人都有自己的长处，应该互相学习。

（三）由

介词“由”跟名词组合，引出动作发出者；也可以在句子中做状语，表示方式、原因或来源。例如：

The preposition “由” is combined with a noun to introduce the agent. It is also used as an adverbial in a sentence to indicate the manner, cause, or source. For example:

1. 我们是由兰笛介绍才认识的。
2. 班长是由全班同学选出来的。
3. 中医认为人的身体是一个由经络和穴位组成的世界。
4. 这次感冒是由天气突然变冷引起的。

（四）从而

连词“从而”用在后一小句的开头，表示结果或进一步的行动。例如：

The conjunction “从而” is used at the beginning of the latter clause to indicate a result or further action. For example:

1. 中医就是用针灸或按摩刺激这些遍布全身的穴位，疏通经络，维持身体各个器官正常的生理功能，从而达到治疗各种疾病的目的。
2. 经济快速发展，社会不断进步，从而为各项事业的发展提供了物质基础。
3. 植树造林，种花种草，从而大大改善了这里的环境。

四 练习 Exercises

（一）朗读 Read aloud

1. 朗读下列发音相近的词语 Read aloud the following words with similar pronunciation

yǒng yòng	yóu yǒng	qíshí	qíshì
有 用	游 泳	其实	歧视

shénqí 神奇	shénqì 神气	wéichí 维持	wèishì 卫士
qìguān 器官	qìguǎn 气管	shēnglǐ 生理	shènglì 胜利

2. 朗读下列短语 Read the following phrases aloud

灵：这个方法很灵　这种药很灵　他的头脑很灵　这个孩子很灵

由：句子由词组成　由你来说明　由老师决定　由班长负责

遍布：遍布全身　遍布全校　遍布全国各地　遍布世界各国

达到：达到治疗疾病的目的　达到提高汉语水平的目的　达到减肥的目的

（二）替换并朗读 Replace and read aloud

1. A：你的腰还疼吗？
   B：不疼了。我的腰早好了。

肚子　头　牙
脖子　腿　手指

2. A：你怎么了？
   B：今天早上一起床，脖子就疼得厉害。

眼睛　背　手
腰　脚　肌肉

3. 我早就听说过中医很神奇。

针灸　按摩　魔术（móshù, magic）
他这个人　西藏

4. 人的身体是由经络和穴位组成的。

我们班　十三个国家的学生
代表团　二十八个人
中华民族　五十六个民族
奥运会的会旗　五个环

（三）**选词填空并朗读下列句子** Choose the appropriate words to fill in the blanks and read aloud the following sentences

总　针　疼　了　怎么　就

1. A：你的腰还________吗？
   B：不疼了，是大夫用针灸给我治好的。
2. A：针灸有那么灵吗？
   B：不信你也试试。你看，我的腰以前________是疼，现在完全好了。
3. 最近，我的腿有点儿疼，我也想去扎扎________。
4. A：今天早上一起床脖子________疼得厉害。
   B：是落枕了。来，你坐下来，我给你按摩按摩。
5. 我按摩以后你就知道________。好，你再抬抬头，动动脖子，看还疼不疼了？
6. 哎，好多了，真的不________疼了，好神奇呀！谢谢大夫！

的　还　什么　了　怎么　又

1. A：戴维，你的脖子好了吗？________疼不疼了？
   B：现在一点儿也不疼了。
2. A：你吃的________药？
   B：我什么药也没吃就好________。
3. A：什么药都没吃？那是________好的？
   B：是大夫给我按摩按好________。
4. A：是吗？按摩有那么灵吗？
   B：开始我也不相信，大夫按摩以后马上就觉得不怎么疼了，我这才相信的。按摩真好，又舒服________治病。

由　认为　其实　从而　遍布　不可思议

1. 我________书上说的不一定都对。
2. 针灸是用针和灸的方法刺激人身上的某个穴位来疏通经络，________达到治疗疾病的目的。
3. 他就是不爱说话，________他是个很好的人。
4. 教育代表团________15 人组成，我们校长是团长。
5. 这家超市________中国各地。
6. 一根针就把我爸爸多年的头疼病治好了，真是让人觉得________。

（四）完成下列句子并大声朗读 Complete the following sentences and read them aloud

1. 几年前我学过一些汉语，但因为不常用，____________________。（完全）
2. 刚来中国时，老师说的话我____________________。（完全）
3. 我的汉语听说能力越来越好，____________________。（从而）
4. 每天做一套练习，____________________。（从而）
5. 都说汉字难，____________________，一年内学习一千五六百个汉字应该没有问题。（其实　只要）
6. 我们都认为昨天和她一起吃饭的那个小伙子是她男朋友，____________________。（其实）
7. 因为晚上睡得太晚，所以，早上____________________。（总）
8. 他们俩是语伴儿，所以，____________________。（总）

（五）完成下列会话并大声朗读 Complete the following conversations and read them aloud

1. A：你的腰还疼吗？
   B：____________________。（一点儿也不）
2. A：你的腰疼是怎么治好的？
   B：____________________。（针灸）

3. A：你的脖子怎么了？
B：________________________________。（落枕）
4. A：你的脖子还疼吗？
B：________________________________。（不……了）
5. A：你的脖子好了？吃的什么药？
B：________________________________。
（什么……也没……）
6. A：按摩有那么灵吗？
B：________________________________。（开始　相信）

（六）和同学一起表演课文会话（一）（二）Act out texts 1 and 2 with your classmates

（七）自由表达 Express yourself freely

跟一个好朋友一起互相做按摩，用汉语说一说是什么感觉：酸（suān, sour）/ 麻（má, numb）/ 胀（zhàng, distended）/ 疼（téng, sore）/ 舒服（shūfu, comfortable）等。

（八）读后说 Read the passage and say it

1. 朗读 Read aloud

我是个幸运儿

我来中国半年多了。我觉得我们班特别好，同学们互相帮助、互相学习，像个大家庭。我们的老师也很好，她处处关心我们，所以，同学们都说她是"老师妈妈"。

我觉得自己是个幸运儿。想起刚来中国时，我一句汉语都不会说，一个汉字都不认识，常常感到很寂寞，想家，还哭过，甚至有点儿后悔来中国留学。可是，不久后，我通过朋友的介绍，认识了一对中国夫妇。他们邀请我去他们家住，我很高兴地答应了。这个家只有叔叔和阿姨两个人，他们的一双儿女都在外国留学。叔叔和阿姨对我非常热情，也非常关心我。有时候我回去得比较晚，但是不管多晚，阿姨都会等我，并为我准备一些好吃的。她对我就像对待自己的亲女儿，使我感到就像在自己家里一样。

为了帮助我尽快提高汉语水平，叔叔给我介绍了一位辅导老师。现在，她成了我最好的中国朋友。她是英语专业的大学生，比我大三岁。她英语说得别提有多好了，还去英国进修过一年。在她的帮助下，我的汉语水平提高得很快。

休息的时候，她常带我出去玩儿，我们一起逛公园、去饭店吃饭、去超市买东西、去电影院看电影、去音乐厅听音乐、去剧院看京剧，我还常跟她和她的朋友们一起用汉语聊天儿。

现在有关学习和生活方面的汉语，我差不多都会说了。我越来越喜欢学习汉语，也越来越习惯这里的生活。我觉得在中国生活很幸福，每天都快快乐乐的。

我打算暑假以后去医科大学学医，所以我要继续努力。

小词典

幸运儿	xìngyùn'ér	名	lucky dog
后悔	hòuhuǐ	动	regret; repent
不久	bùjiǔ	形	soon; before long
答应	dāying	动	agree
亲	qīn	形	related by blood or marriage
尽快	jǐnkuài	副	as quickly (soon or early) as possible
辅导	fǔdǎo	动	tutor; give guidance in study or training
进修	jìnxiū	动	(often on leave from one's position for a set time) engage in advanced studies
剧院	jùyuàn	名	theater

2. 朗读下列问句并回答 Read aloud the following interrogative sentences and answer them

（1）“我”来中国多长时间了？

（2）“我们”班怎么样？

（3）“我”刚来中国时是什么情况？

（4）“我”是怎么住到中国人家里去的？

（5）叔叔和阿姨对“我”怎么样？

（6）“我”有没有中国朋友？

（7）“我”的汉语说得好吗？“我”是怎么学的？

（8）“我”打算继续在这里学下去吗？

3. 你是A，请你向B提问 Supposing you are A, ask B questions

（1）A：________________________________？（多长）

B：我来中国半年多了。

（2）A：________________________________？（多少）

B：我们班有18个学生。

（3）A：________________________________？（怎么样）

B：我觉得我们班特别好，同学们互相帮助、互相学习，像个大家庭。

（4）A：________________________________？（什么　感觉）

B：刚来中国时，我一句汉语都不会说，常常感到很寂寞，想家，甚至还有点儿后悔来中国留学。

（5）A：________________________________？（什么　情况）

B：家里只有叔叔和阿姨两个人，他们的一双儿女都在外国留学。叔叔和阿姨对我非常热情，也非常关心我。有时候我回去得比较晚，但是不管多晚，阿姨都会等我，并为我准备一些好吃的。她对我就像对待自己的亲女儿，使我感到就像在自己家里一样。

（6）A：________________________？（做　什么）

B：休息的时候她常带我出去玩儿，我们一起逛公园、去饭店吃饭、去商店买东西、去电影院看电影，还常跟她和她的朋友们一起用汉语聊天儿。

（7）A：________________________？（什么　打算）

B：我打算暑假以后去医科大学学医，所以我要继续努力。

4. 复述这篇课文 Retell this text

（九）朗读中国经典诗词，请注意语音语调 Read aloud the classic Chinese poem and pay attention to the pronunciation and intonation

Tí Xīlín Bì
题西林壁

[Sòng] Sū Shì
[宋] 苏 轼（1037—1101）

Héng kàn chéng lǐng cè chéng fēng, yuǎn jìn gāo dī gè bù tóng.
横看成岭侧成峰，远近高低各不同。

Bù shí Lú Shān zhēn miànmù, zhǐ yuán shēn zài cǐ shān zhōng.
不识庐山真面目，只缘身在此山中。

（十）请欣赏下列著名的词句 Please enjoy the following famous saying

Liángyào kǔkǒu lìyú bìng, zhōngyán nì'ěr lìyú xíng.
良药苦口利于病，忠言逆耳利于行。

Good medicine tastes bitter,
and honest advice is unpleasant to hear.

Dì-wǔshíyī kè Zuówǎn de zúqiúsài nǐ kànle ma

第五十一课 昨晚的足球赛你看了吗

Lesson 51 Did you watch the soccer game last night?

一 课文 Text

A：昨晚的足球赛你看了吗？

B：看了。你呢？

A：我只看了前半场，后来朋友突然病了，我送他去医院，就没看完。最后谁赢了？

B：黑虎队。

A：怎么是黑虎队赢了？几比几？

B：3 比 1。

A：我看前半场红牛队 1 比 0 领先着呢，怎么下半场让人家连进三个球？黑虎队怎么这么厉害？

B：黑虎队请了一个著名的教练，水平提高得很快，可以说是突飞猛进。

A：红牛队是怎么搞的，这么不争气！他们也太大意了。

B：看来黑虎队实力还是比红牛队强。红牛队前锋队员的临门一脚，老是欠点儿火候，整体配合也有些问题。后半场踢得一点儿章法都没有。快终场时，红牛队的 9 号又在禁区故意推人，吃了一张红牌儿，被罚下场，让黑虎队赢得了一个点球。最后以 3 比 1 锁定了胜局。

A：真是的。这叫什么事儿嘛！真让人泄气。

B：不过，红牛队的守门员表现不错，扑住了好几个险球，要不输得更惨。

二 生词 New Words

1	足球赛	zúqiúsài	名	soccer game
	赛	sài	动	game; match
2	虎	hǔ	名	tiger
3	领先	lǐng xiān	动	lead; be in the lead
4	著名	zhùmíng	形	famous
5	教练	jiàoliàn	名	coach
6	提高	tí gāo	动	raise; improve
7	突飞猛进	tūfēi-měngjìn		(of a cause, learning, etc.) advance by leaps and bounds
8	大意	dàyi	形	careless
9	实力	shílì	名	actual strength; power
10	强	qiáng	形	strong; powerful
11	前锋	qiánfēng	名	(in basketball, soccer, etc.) forward; player whose task is to attack or score
12	队员	duìyuán	名	team member
13	临门一脚	línmén yì jiǎo		go for the goal
	临门	línmén	动	face the goal
14	老是	lǎoshì	副	always; all the time
15	欠	qiàn	动	not enough
16	火候	huǒhou	名	level of accomplishment or sophistication

17 整体	zhěngtǐ	名	whole; entirety
18 配合	pèihé	动	coordinate; cooperate
19 章法	zhāngfǎ	名	methodicalness
20 终场	zhōngchǎng	动	end (of a performance or game)
21 禁区	jìnqū	名	penalty area (in certain types of ball games)
22 故意	gùyì	副	on purpose; consciously
23 吃	chī	动	suffer; incur; bear
24 红牌儿	hóngpáir	名	red card
25 罚	fá	动	punish
26 赢得	yíngdé	动	win; gain
27 点球	diǎnqiú	名	penalty kick
28 以	yǐ	介、连	with; by means of
29 锁定	suǒdìng	动	(of a game) be in the bag
30 胜局	shèngjú	名	victory; success
31 泄气	xiè qì	动	lose heart; feel discouraged
32 守门员	shǒuményuán	名	goalkeeper
33 扑	pū	动	(of a soccer game) save (a goal)
34 险	xiǎn	形	dangerous
35 要不	yàobù	连	otherwise; or else; or
36 输	shū	动	lose (in a game)
37 惨	cǎn	形	serious; calamitous

三 注释 Notes

（一）连

副词“连”表示连续，用在动词前面做状语，动词后边常带数量词。例如：

The adverb “连” is used as an adverbial before a verb to indicate continuity. The verb is often followed by a quantifier. For example:

1. 我看前半场红牛队1比0领先着呢，怎么下半场让人家连进三个球？
2. 连下了两场雪，气温一下子降了下来。
3. 我给他连发了三个短信，他都没有回。

（二）老是

“老是”表示“经常是，常常是”，多用于对某人或某事的主观评价，常带有不满情绪。例如：

“老是” means “often”. It is often used to make subjective assessment of somebody or something with a sense of dissatisfaction. For example:

1. 红牛队前锋队员的临门一脚，老是欠点儿火候，整体配合也有些问题。
2. 你怎么老是迟到，我都等你半个小时了。
3. 这里的气候老是这么干燥（gānzào, dry）。
4. 这几天老是下雨，下得人心烦。

（三）以

“以”是介词，有“用，拿”的意思，在句子中做状语。例如：

The preposition “以” means “with” and is used as an adverbial in a sentence. For example:

1. 快终场时，红牛队的9号又在禁区故意推人，让黑虎队赢得了一个点球，最后以3比1锁定胜局。
2. 黑虎队中间还被罚下场了一个人，可是最后还是以少胜多。
3. 他们打算以新产品替代老产品。

（四）真是的

"真是的"也说"真是"，表示"实在是"，口语中常常用"真是的"表示不满的情绪和语气。例如：

"真是的" is also abbreviated as "真是", which means "indeed". It is often used in spoken Chinese to show dissatisfaction. For example:

1. A：快终场时，红牛队的 9 号又在禁区故意推人，让黑虎队赢得了一个点球，最后以 3 比 1 锁定胜局。

   B：真是的。

2. 真是的，这么一点儿事你都办不成。
3. 这天，真是的，老刮风。

（五）要不

"要不"表示"不然""要不是这样的话"，用在第二个分句前面。例如：

"要不" means "otherwise, or". It is used before the second clause. For example:

1. 红牛队的守门员表现不错，扑住了好几个险球，要不输得更惨。
2. 这个星期六我们去爬山吧，要不就去游泳。
3. 你还是跟他道个歉吧，要不他肯定生气。
4. 我们坐车去吧，要不就骑车去，反正也不远。

四 练习 Exercises

（一）朗读 Read aloud

1. 朗读下列发音相近的词语 Read aloud the following words with similar pronunciation

zhēng qì 争气	zhèngqì 正气	zhěngtǐ 整体	zhěngqí 整齐
zhōngchǎng 终场	zhōngcháng 衷肠	jìnqū 禁区	jìnqǔ 进取
shèngjú 胜局	shèngjǔ 盛举	biǎoxiàn 表现	bǎoxiǎn 保险

2. 朗读下列短语 Read the following phrases aloud

半：半场　半天　半年　半个月　半个小时

连：连胜三场　连下了两天雪　连得三分　连输了五个球

著名：著名教练　著名导演　著名演员　著名作家　著名球星

争气：不争气　真争气　争气的孩子　要争一口气

章法：没有章法　很有章法　要有章法

以：以3比1锁定胜局　以点球决定胜负　以点球取胜　以少胜多

（二）替换并朗读 Replace and read aloud

1. 昨天晚上的足球赛你看了吗？

排球赛	篮球赛
网球赛	乒乓球赛
游泳比赛	体操比赛

2. A：怎么是黑虎队赢了？几比几？
   B：3比1。

3比2	3比0
4比1	5比3
110比86	

3. 红牛队是怎么搞的，这么不争气！

这么没水平	踢得这么不好
真让人生气	踢得这么糟糕

4. 看来黑虎队实力还是比红牛队强。

这个房间	那个	暖和
你的车	我的	高级
这种手机	那种	好
微信	伊妹儿	方便得多
国产的	进口的	好用

5. 老是欠点儿火候。

踢不进去	没有精神	迟到
一上课就犯困		感冒

（三）**选词填空并朗读下列句子** Choose the appropriate words to fill in the blanks and read aloud the following sentences

教练　比　搞　了　老　要不　吃　这么

1. A：昨晚的足球赛你看________吗？
   B：我只看了前半场，后来朋友突然病了，我送他去医院，就没看完，最后谁赢了？
2. A：黑虎队赢了。
   B：怎么是黑虎队赢了？几________几？
3. 我看前半场红牛队 1 比 0 领先着呢，怎么下半场让人家连进三个球？黑虎队怎么________厉害？
4. 黑虎队请了一个著名________，这两年水平提高得很快，可以说是突飞猛进。
5. 红牛队是怎么________的，这么不争气！
6. 看来黑虎队实力还是比红牛队强。红牛队前锋队员的临门一脚，________是欠点儿火候，整体配合也有些问题。
7. 快终场时，红牛队的 9 号又在禁区故意推人，________了一张红牌儿，被罚下场，让黑虎队赢得了一个点球。最后以 3 比 1 锁定了胜局。
8. 红牛队的守门员表现不错，扑住了好几个险球，________输得更惨。

整体　大意　赢得　火候　泄气　争气　半　连

1. 你去哪儿了，让我找了你________天。

2. 他________考了三年才考上这所著名的大学。
3. 他们真不________，这次又输了。
4. 他汉语说得还可以，就是声调还欠点儿________。
5. 他们队的________配合有问题，场上踢得很乱。
6. 快到终场的时候，8号在禁区故意推人，结果让对方________了一个点球。
7. 路上一定要小心，千万不能________。
8. 遇到再大的困难也不要________，要通过自己的努力取得成功。

（四）**完成下列句子并大声朗读** Complete the following sentences and read them aloud

1. 不知道为什么，最近他________________。（老是）
2. 昨天晚上我躺在床上，________________。（老是）
3. 我发现你________________就去上课，这样怎么行？（老是）
4. 最让人看不起的就是，一些足球队员________________。（故意）
5. 不小心踩了别人的脚，虽然________________，还是应该向人家说声"对不起"。（故意）
6. 你不要怪他，我想他________________。（故意）
7. 我们去游泳吧，________________。（要不）
8. 咱们去听音乐会吧，________________。（要不）

（五）**完成下列会话并大声朗读** Complete the following conversations and read them aloud

1. A：昨晚的足球赛你看了吗？
   B：________________________________。
2. A：我只看了前半场，后来朋友突然病了，我送他去医院，就没看完。最后谁赢了？
   B：________________________________。（黑虎队）
3. A：怎么是黑虎队赢了？几比几？
   B：________________________________。（比）

4. A：我看前半场红牛队1比0领先着呢，怎么下半场让人家连进三个球？黑虎队怎么这么厉害？

B：________________________________。

（著名教练　突飞猛进）

5. A：红牛队真是的！真让人泄气！

B：________________________________。

（不过　守门员　要不）

（六）**和同学一起表演课文** Act out the text with your classmates

（七）**自由表达** Express yourself freely

和同学一起看一次足球赛，用汉语说说比赛的情况：比赛的是哪两个队？哪个球员踢得好？比赛结果是多少？

（八）**读后说** Read the passage and say it

1. 朗读 Read aloud

曹冲称象

这是东汉（25—220）末年的故事。

当时中国北方没有大象，南方吴地送给当时掌权的曹操一头大象，曹操十分高兴。

大象运来的那天，曹操和大臣们都来观看。曹操对大家说："这头象又高又大，你们谁有办法称一称它的重量？"

这么个大家伙，怎么称呢？大臣们纷纷议论开了。一个说："只有造一杆很大的秤才能称。"另一个说："这要造多大的秤呀！再说，大象是活的，也没办法称呀！我看只有把它杀了，切成块儿称。"他的话刚说完，有人就说："你这算什么办法呀！为了称重量，就把大象杀了，这怎么行呢？"

大臣们想来想去，都想不出什么好办法。

这时，一个七岁的小男孩儿站出来对曹操说："爸爸，我有办法，可以称出大象的重量。"

曹操一看，是自己的小儿子曹冲，就笑着说："你小小年纪，能有什么办法？你说说，让我听听有没有道理。"

曹冲说了自己的办法，曹操一听连连叫好，吩咐人按照曹冲的办法称象。他对大臣们说："走！咱们到河边儿看称象去！"

大臣们跟随曹操来到河边儿，河里停着一只大船。曹冲叫人把象牵到船上，等船不动的时候，在水面到达船身的地方做了一个记号，再叫人把象牵到岸上来。然后，把大大小小的石头，一块一块地搬到船上去，船身一点儿一点儿往下沉，等船身沉到刚才刻的那个记号时，曹冲就叫人停止装石头。

大臣们看到这里才明白过来，不由得称赞说："好办法！好办法！只要把船里的石头称一下，就知道大象有多重了。"

小词典

称	chēng	动	weigh
（大）象	(dà) xiàng	名	elephant
当时	dāngshí	名	at that time
掌权	zhǎng quán	动	be in power
十分	shífēn	副	very
重量	zhòngliàng	名	weight
大臣	dàchén	名	minister
纷纷	fēnfēn	副	one after another
议论	yìlùn	动、名	discuss; comment
家伙	jiāhuo	名	guy
造	zào	动	make
杆	gǎn	量	*a measure word for implements with a shaft*
秤	chèng	名	balance; steelyard

杀	shā	动	kill
切	qiē	动	cut
吩咐	fēnfù	动	order; tell
跟随	gēnsuí	动	follow
牵	qiān	动	lead along
稳定	wěndìng	形	stable; steady
记号	jìhao	名	mark; sign
石头	shítou	名	stone
沉	chén	动、形	sink; heavy
不由得	bùyóude	动、副	cannot help
称赞	chēngzàn	动	praise

专名

东汉	Dōng Hàn	Eastern Han Dynasty
曹操	Cáo Cāo（155—220）	name of a person
曹冲	Cáo Chōng（196—208）	name of a person

2. 回答下列问题 Answer the following questions

（1）中国的北方有没有大象？

（2）谁送给曹操一只大象？

（3）曹操对大臣们说了什么？

（4）大臣们有哪些称象的办法？

（5）谁想出来了一个称象的好办法？

（6）曹冲是怎么称象的？

3. 你是 A，请你向 B 提问 Supposing you are A, ask B questions

（1）A：______________________________？（大象　吗）

B：当时中国的北方没有大象。

（2）A: ________________？（曹操　什么）
B: 曹操对大家说："这只象又高又大，你们谁有办法称一称它的重量？"

（3）A: ________________？（大臣　什么）
B: 有人说要造一杆很大的秤来称，也有人说把大象杀了，切成块儿称。

（4）A: ________________？（谁）
B: 曹操的儿子曹冲有个好办法能称出大象的重量。

（5）A: ________________？（曹冲　怎么　称）
B: 曹冲叫人把大象牵到船上，等船不动的时候，在水面达到船身的地方做了一个记号，再叫人把大象牵到岸上来。然后，把大大小小的石头，一块一块地搬到船上去，船身一点儿一点儿往下沉，等船身沉到刚才刻的那个记号时，曹冲就叫人停止装石头。只要把船里的石头称一下，就知道大象有多重了。

4. 复述这篇课文 Retell this text

（九）朗读中国经典诗词，请注意语音语调 Read aloud the classic Chinese poem and pay attention to the pronunciation and intonation

Jiāngnán Chūn
江南　春

[Táng] Dù Mù
［唐］杜牧（803—853）

Qiān lǐ yīng tí lǜ yìng hóng, shuǐ cūn shān guō jiǔ qí fēng.
千里莺啼绿映红，水村山郭酒旗风。
Nán Cháo sìbǎi bāshí sì, duōshǎo lóutái yānyǔ zhōng.
南朝四百八十寺，多少楼台烟雨中。

（十）请欣赏下列著名的词句 Please enjoy the following famous saying

Fùguì bù néng yín, pínjiàn bù néng yí, wēiwǔ bù néng qū.

富贵不能淫，贫贱不能移，威武不能屈。

For a great man, neither riches nor honors can corrupt him,

neither poverty nor humbleness can make him swerve from principles,

and neither threats nor forces can subdue him.

Dì-wǔshí'èr kè　　Yèyú shíjiān nǐ zuò shénme

第五十二课　业余时间你做什么

Lesson 52　What do you do in your spare time?

一　课文 Text

（一）我的业余生活很丰富

（两个留学生在谈自己的业余生活）

松山：除了上课以外，业余时间你常做什么？

河野：我的业余生活很丰富，总觉得时间不够用。

松山：你都干什么呀？

河野：学太极拳、学书画、学弹琵琶、学拉二胡、学做中国菜，我还参加了一个环保志愿者组织，和中国大学生一起搞环保宣传，为保护环境尽一点儿力。

松山：啊，你活动可真够多的，忙得过来吗？

河野：忙是忙了点儿，可是我觉得非常充实和愉快。

松山：你的时间是怎么安排的？

河野：我每天早上学打太极拳，每星期二下午学书法和中国画，星期五晚上学弹琵琶或拉二胡，周六去参加环保志愿者活动。

松山：不累吗？安排得这么满！

河野：不觉得累，倒觉得很有意思。尤其是参加环保志愿者组织，让我结识了很多中国大学生。了解了他们，和他们成了朋友，同时也提高了我的汉语水平，丰富了自己的人生经验。你呢？你业余时间是怎么安排的？

松山：我呀，我跟朋友一起在网上办了一份杂志。

河野：什么杂志？

松山：是介绍中国饮食文化的杂志，目的是向我们国家介绍中国菜。所以，我得常常下馆子，吃中国菜，还要采访一些经验丰富的厨师。点了菜以后，得先给每个菜拍照、拍视频，回来以后还要写解说词，介绍每个菜的材料、做法、味道等等。我几乎吃遍了这里所有的饭店，都快成美食家了。

河野：那多好啊，每天都吃好吃的！

松山：好是好，可你没发现吗？我越来越胖了。

（二）丹尼丝的生日晚会我可能参加不了

（美穗因为不能参加同学的生日晚会，向班长请假）

美穗：班长，对不起，丹尼丝的生日晚会我可能参加不了。

班长：为什么？

美穗：我晚上有课。

班长：有课？什么课？

美穗：今天晚上我要跟老师学习拉二胡。

班长：难怪我们班几次活动都见不着你。

美穗：对不起，除了星期六和星期日以外，平时我每天下午或晚上都有自己的安排。星期一学习书法和中国画，星期二要跟中国语伴儿互教互学，一起练口语，星期三学唱京剧，星期四是中华料理课，星期五学拉二胡。

班长：你业余生活真丰富啊。

美穗：是啊，来一次中国不容易，我想多学点儿东西。我的理想是当中文老师。你知道，要当老师除了学好汉语，还得了解中国，有丰富的中华文化知识。

班长：你不参加，大家会感到遗憾的。

美穗：对不起。我这里有一份礼物，麻烦你转交给丹尼丝，祝她生日快乐。

二 生词 New Words

1	业余	yèyú	形	amateur
2	环保	huánbǎo	名、形	environmental protection; eco-friendly
3	宣传	xuānchuán	动	publicize
4	保护	bǎohù	动	protect
5	环境	huánjìng	名	environment
6	安排	ānpái	动	arrange; plan
7	倒	dào	副	*contrary to what is expected or thought*
8	尤其	yóuqí	副	especially; particularly
9	结识	jiéshí	动	get acquainted with sb.; get to know sb.
10	同时	tóngshí	连、名	at the same time; contemporay
11	经验	jīngyàn	名	experience
12	份	fèn	量	*a measure word for newspapers or magazines*
13	饮食	yǐnshí	名	food and drink; diet
14	馆子	guǎnzi	名	restaurant; eatery
15	厨师	chúshī	名	cook
16	解说词	jiěshuōcí	名	(written) caption; (oral) commentary
	解说	jiěshuō	动	explain orally
17	材料	cáiliào	名	material
18	做法	zuòfǎ	名	way of doing or making sth.
19	几乎	jīhū	副	nearly; almost
20	遍	biàn	动	all over; everywhere
21	美食家	měishíjiā	名	gourmet

22 发现	fāxiàn	动	discover; find
23 晚会	wǎnhuì	名	party; gala
24 平时	píngshí	名	ordinary times; normal times
25 互	hù	副	mutually
26 料理	liàolǐ	名、动	food and drink; cusine; cook
27 知识	zhīshi	名	knowledge
28 礼物	lǐwù	名	gift; present
29 转交	zhuǎnjiāo	动	pass on to

专名 Zhuānmíng Proper Nouns

1 中华	Zhōnghuá	China
2 河野	Héyě	name of a person
3 美穗	Měisuì	name of a person

三 注释 Notes

（一）尤其

"尤其"表示在全体中或与其他事物比较时更加突出，更进一步。例如：

"尤其" indicates that something or somebody is more prominent and progressive than the other in a group or in comparison with others. For example:

1. 不觉得累，倒觉得很有意思。尤其是参加环保志愿者组织，让我结识了很多中国大学生。了解了他们，和他们成了朋友，也提高了我的汉语水平。
2. 北京有很多很美的公园，尤其是颐和园，最美。
3. 我们班的同学学习都很努力，尤其是玛丽，特别努力。
4. 公园里什么时候人都很多，尤其是节假日，人就更多了。

（二）几乎

副词“几乎”表示十分接近、差不多的意思。例如：

The adverb “几乎” means “very close, almost”. For example:

1. 我们大学的留学生几乎有一万人。
2. 这幅画儿和真的几乎一模一样。

四 练习 Exercises

（一）朗读 Read aloud

1. 朗读下列发音相近的词语 Read aloud the following words with similar pronunciation

fēngfù 丰富	fēnfù 吩咐	huánbǎo 环保	huánbào 环抱
yóuqí 尤其	yóuqī 油漆	jiéshí 结识	jiěshì 解释
jiànlì 建立	jiǎnlì 简历	chúshī 厨师	chū shì 出 事

2. 朗读下列短语 Read the following phrases aloud

丰富：经验丰富　知识丰富　业余生活很丰富　丰富了人生经验

环保：环保工作　环保工作者　环保志愿者

宣传：大力宣传　宣传环保　宣传群众

安排：安排工作　工作安排　安排活动

尤其：尤其好看　尤其漂亮　尤其重要　尤其喜欢

提高：提高水平　提高质量　提高听说能力　提高读写能力

采访：采访厨师　采访教授　采访演员　去中国采访

遍：走遍了　吃遍了　看遍了　玩儿遍了
再看一遍　再听一遍　再说一遍　再预习一遍
再复习一遍

互：互教互学　互帮互学　互谅互让　互敬互爱

（二）替换并朗读 Replace and read aloud

1. 我还参加了一个志愿者组织，和中国大学生一起，为环境保护工作尽一点儿力。

老年人事业	农村教育
保护未成年人事业	保护动物
科普（kēpǔ, popular science）事业	

2. 忙是忙了点儿，可是我觉得非常充实和愉快。

累是累	难是难	苦是苦

3. 我跟朋友一起办了一份杂志。

一份报纸	一个公司
一个读书会	一个网站

4. 目的是向我们国家介绍中国菜，所以，我得常常下馆子，吃中国菜，还要采访厨师。

中国京剧	去剧场	看京剧	演员
中医	去中医院	看针灸按摩	中医大夫
中国功夫	去武术馆	看表演	武术教练和运动员
中国音乐	去音乐厅	听音乐	音乐家

5. 我几乎吃遍了这里所有的中国饭店，都快成美食家了。

走	中国的名山	旅行家
看	中国的新电影	影迷
听	中国的新民歌	歌迷
拍	中国的建筑	摄影家

6. 那多好啊，每天都<u>吃好吃的</u>！

喝好喝的　看好看的
听好听的　玩儿好玩儿的

7. 我这里有一份礼物，麻烦你转交给她，祝她<u>生日快乐</u>。

节日快乐　万事如意
早日康复　考上一个好大学

（三）**选词填空并朗读下列句子** Choose the appropriate words to fill in the blanks and read aloud the following sentences

过来　为　意思　份　参加　除了

1. A：________上课外，业余时间你常做什么？
   B：我的业余生活很丰富，总觉得时间不够用。
2. 学太极拳、学书画、学弹琵琶、学拉二胡、学做中国菜，我还参加了一个环保志愿者组织，和中国大学生一起搞环保宣传，________保护环境尽一点儿力。
3. A：啊，你活动可真够多的，忙得________吗？
   B：忙是忙了点儿，可是我觉得非常充实和愉快。
4. 我星期五晚上学弹琵琶或拉二胡，周六去________环保志愿者活动。
5. 我不觉得累，倒觉得很有________。尤其是参加环保志愿者组织，让我结识了很多中国大学生。了解了他们，和他们成了朋友，同时也提高了我的汉语水平，丰富了自己的人生经验。
6. 我跟朋友一起在网上办了一________杂志，是介绍中国饮食文化的，目的是向我们国家介绍中国菜。

跟　的　遗憾　参加　着　祝　多

1. 班长，对不起，丹尼丝的生日晚会我________不了。

2. A：为什么？

B：今天晚上我要________老师学习拉二胡。

3. 难怪我们班几次活动都见不________你。

4. 对不起，除了星期六和星期日以外，平时我每天下午或晚上都有自己________安排。来一次中国不容易，我想________学点儿东西。我的理想是当中文老师。你知道，要当老师除了学好汉语，还得了解中国，有丰富的中华文化知识。

5. 你不参加，大家会感到________的。

6. 对不起。我这里有一份礼物，麻烦你转交给丹尼丝，________她生日快乐。

保护　环境　提高　充实　结识　志愿者

1. 我参加了一个环保志愿者组织，想为保护________尽点儿力。

2. 我们的社会因为有这些________而变得更加美好。

3. 让我们行动起来，一起________我们人类共同的家园——地球。

4. 当你为大家的事情而努力的时候，你就会感到自己的生活非常________。

5. 我来中国快一年了，________了很多朋友。

6. 要想很快地________汉语听说水平，就要多跟中国人交谈。

（四）用“几乎”完成下列句子并大声朗读 Complete the following sentences with “几乎” and read them aloud

1. 这个电视节目我____________________，越看越有意思。

2. 汽车越来越多，一到假期，公路____________________。

3. 来中国以后，做饭、做菜、洗衣服，我____________________。

4. 我只想着跟朋友聊天了，____________________。

5. 这次听力考试比较难，我____________________。

6. 我喜欢这些古诗，有一些我____________________。（背）

（五）完成下列会话并大声朗读 Complete the following conversations and read them aloud

1. A：你的业余生活怎么样？

   B：________________________________。

（丰富　总　时间）

2. A：除了上课以外，你业余时间常做什么？

   B：________________________________。

（太极拳　书画　中国菜　拉二胡　环保志愿者）

3. A：你活动可真够多的，忙得过来吗？

   B：________________________________。

（忙是忙　觉得　充实　愉快）

4. A：你的时间是怎么安排的？

   B：________________________________。

（每天　星期二　星期三　星期六）

5. A：不累吗？安排得这么满！

   B：________________________________。

（觉得　倒　有意思　尤其是）

6. A：一年来，我几乎吃遍了这里所有的中国饭店，都快成美食家了。

   B：那多好啊，每天都吃好吃的！

   A：________________________________。

（好是好　越来越）

7. A：今天晚上的活动你能参加吗？

   B：对不起，____________________。

8. A：你不来大家会感到遗憾的。

   B：________________________________。

（礼物　转交）

（六）和同学一起表演课文 Act out the text with your classmates

（七）自由表达 Express yourself freely

和一两个好朋友一起，互相一问一答，说说自己的业余生活：看了什么书？拍了哪些照片？录了什么好节目？参加了什么体育活动？画了什么画儿？练习了什么书法？做了什么菜？参加了什么社团活动？等等。

（八）读后说 Read the passage and say it

1. 朗读 Read aloud

寻找幸福

一天课间休息的时候，老师对我们说，咱们做个游戏吧，大家都说好。老师给我们班上的 20 多个同学每人发了一个气球。他要我们每个人都把气球充好气，并在上面写上自己的名字，然后再把气球放到走廊里。接着，老师把 20 多个气球混合在一起，让我们在五分钟内，从走廊里的气球堆中找出写着自己名字的那个气球。

老师一说开始，我们就急忙去找。尽管我们的动作很快，但几乎没有人能在五分钟内找到写着自己名字的气球。

这时，老师告诉我们，如果我们很快拿起一个气球，把它交给写着名字的人，可能不到五分钟，我们每个人就都能拿到自己的气球了。

大家试了一下，果然，我们很快就拿到了写有自己名字的气球。

最后，老师语重心长地对大家说："这些气球就像幸福，如果每个人都只寻找自己的幸福，我们可能很难找到幸福；但如果我们都关心他人的幸福，帮助他人得到幸福，那么我们自己也会得到幸福。幸福，其实就是个人的一种感觉！我们常说助人为乐，帮助他人时自己获得快乐的感觉，就是幸福啊！"

老师的话，让我们陷入了沉思。

小词典

寻找	xúnzhǎo	动	look for; search
课间	kèjiān	名	break (between classes)

气球	qìqiú	名	balloon
走廊	zǒuláng	名	corridor
混合	hùnhé	动	mix; mingle
急忙	jímáng	副	hastily; hurriedly; in a hurry
尽管	jǐnguǎn	副、连	though; although
果然	guǒrán	副	sure enough; really
语重心长	yǔzhòng-xīncháng		(say sth.) in all earnestness
陷入	xiànrù	动	be caught in
沉思	chénsī	动	ruminate; contemplate

2. 朗读下列问句并回答 Read aloud the following interrogative sentences and answer the questions

（1）这天课间休息的时候，老师要同学们做什么？
（2）老师给同学们发了一个什么东西？
（3）老师要同学们给气球充气后，在气球上写什么？
（4）同学们把气球堆放在了什么地方？
（5）老师喊开始后，让同学们找什么？
（6）老师要求同学们在多长时间内找到写有自己名字的气球？
（7）同学们在五分钟内找到写有自己名字的气球了吗？
（8）后来同学们是怎样很快地找到写有自己名字的气球的？
（9）老师把气球比成了什么？
（10）你觉得这个游戏有意思吗？

3. 你是 A，请你向 B 提问 Supposing you are A, ask B questions

（1）A：________________________？（做什么）
B：一天课间休息的时候，老师对我们说，咱们做个游戏吧。
（2）A：________________________？
B：老师给我们班上的 20 多个同学每人发了一个气球。

（3）A：________________________？（写什么）

B：他要我们每个人都把气球充好气，并在上面写上自己的名字。

（4）A：________________________？（找什么）

B：老师把 20 多个气球混合在一起，要我们在走廊的气球堆中找出写着自己名字的那个气球。

（5）A：________________________？（多长时间）

B：他让我们在五分钟内找到。

（6）A：________________________？（怎么）

B：老师一说开始，我们就急忙去找。

（7）A：________________________？

B：尽管我们的动作很快，但几乎没有人能在五分钟内找到自己的气球。

（8）A：________________________？（怎么　找到）

B：老师告诉我们，如果我们很快拿起一个气球，把它交给写着名字的人，可能不到五分钟，我们每个人就都能拿到自己的气球了。

（9）A：________________________？（结果）

B：大家试了一下，果然，我们很快就拿到了写有自己名字的气球。

（10）A：________________________？（像　什么）

B：老师语重心长地对我们说："这些气球就像幸福，如果每个人都只寻找自己的幸福，我们可能很难找到幸福；但如果我们都关心他人的幸福，帮助他人得到幸福，那么我们也会得到自己的幸福。"

4. 复述这篇课文 Retell this text

（九）朗读中国经典诗词，请注意语音语调 Read aloud the classic Chinese poem and pay attention to the pronunciation and intonation

Yǐn Húshàng Chū Qíng Hòu Yǔ
饮 湖上 初 晴 后 雨

[Sòng] Sū Shì
[宋] 苏 轼（1037—1101）

Shuǐguāng liànyàn qíng fāng hǎo, shānsè kōngméng yǔ yì qí.
水光 潋滟 晴 方 好，山色 空濛 雨 亦奇。
Yù bǎ Xī Hú bǐ Xīzǐ, dàn zhuāng nóng mǒ zǒng xiāngyí.
欲把西湖比西子，淡 妆 浓 抹 总 相宜。

（十）请欣赏下列著名的词句 Please enjoy the following famous saying

Zhìzhě bú huò, rénzhě bù yōu, yǒngzhě bú jù.
知者 不 惑，仁者 不 忧，勇者 不惧。

The wise are free from puzzles,
the virtuous are free from worries,
and the brave are free from fears.

Dì-wǔshísān kè　Zhù nǐ shēngrì kuàilè

第五十三课　祝你生日快乐

Lesson 53　Happy birthday to you

一　课文 Text

（一）咱们把客厅布置布置吧

（晚上要在客厅为丹尼丝举行生日晚会，罗兰和山本要把客厅布置布置）

山本：今晚要在这儿为丹尼丝开生日晚会，咱们把客厅布置布置吧。

罗兰：怎么布置？你说吧，我和你一起干。

山本：先把这些乱七八糟的东西收拾一下。

罗兰：你看，把这两张桌子对在一起，摆在中间，把椅子放在四周，怎么样？

山本：行。这桌子上也太乱了，把这些画报、杂志放到什么地方去呢？

罗兰：把不用的东西先收起来，再把桌子擦擦，把我这块儿花布铺上吧。

山本：把我们买的那束鲜花插在花瓶里，放在桌子上吧。

罗兰：这样差不多了吧？

山本：地板有点儿脏，你把墩布递给我，我再把地板拖一拖。

罗兰：你累了，休息一会儿吧，让我来。

山本：好了。这一收拾，客厅里显得又干净又整齐。

（二）祝你生日快乐

（同学们在为丹尼丝过生日）

山　本：丹尼丝，生日快乐！

丹尼丝：谢谢！

山　本：把蜡烛插在蛋糕上吧。

罗　兰：插多少支呢？

山　本：应该插二十支，二十岁了嘛。好，请寿星把蜡烛点上吧。哎，打火机呢？（对罗兰）我把打火机弄哪儿去了？

罗　兰：别找了，在这儿。

（丹尼丝接过打火机，点蜡烛）

罗　兰：把灯关上吧？

山　本：关上吧。来，让我们祝丹尼丝生日快乐。

（大家一齐唱：祝你生日快乐，祝你生日快乐……）

山　本：好。该寿星许愿了。

（丹尼丝在默默许愿）

山　本：该吹蜡烛了。丹尼丝，要是一口气把蜡烛全吹灭，你许的愿就都能实现。

丹尼丝：真的吗？那我可得加把劲儿。

（丹尼丝吹灭了蜡烛，大家一起鼓掌，罗兰把灯打开）

山　本：请寿星来切蛋糕吧。

丹尼丝：切多少块呢？

山　本：一、二、三……把它切成二十块吧，我们一共二十个人。

马　丁：丹尼丝，你刚才许的什么愿哪？是不是希望快点儿找个男朋友？

丹尼丝：不告诉你。

罗　兰：（对大伙儿）快，来吃蛋糕了。马丁，给，快吃蛋糕吧。

马　丁：谢谢！

（三）我去参加朋友的生日晚会了

A：昨天晚上你去哪儿了？手机还关机了，我去找你，你不在。

B：昨晚丹尼丝过生日，我去参加她的生日晚会了。

A：怎么样？

B：可热闹了，我们班大部分同学都去了。大家又说又笑，一起吃蛋糕、一起唱歌。因为是第一次在中国过生日，所以她特别高兴。你看，这是我给她拍的照片。

A：真漂亮！她身边怎么那么多玩具小狗啊？

B：这是同学们送给她的生日礼物，因为丹尼丝是属于狗的。

A：不能这么说，要说她是属狗的。

B：是吗？我常常说错了。

A：“常常”后面不能有“了”。

B：啊，我常常说错，这次我记住了。

二 生词 New Words

1	椅子	yǐzi	名	chair
2	四周	sìzhōu	名	all around; on all sides
3	擦	cā	动	wipe
4	铺	pū	动	spread
5	布	bù	名	cloth
6	插	chā	动	insert
7	花瓶	huāpíng	名	vase
8	地板	dìbǎn	名	floor
9	脏	zāng	形	dirty; unclean
10	墩布	dūnbù	名	mop; swab
11	拖	tuō	动	mop
12	显得	xiǎnde	动	look; seem; appear
13	蜡烛	làzhú	名	candle
14	点	diǎn	动	light (a fire)
15	打火机	dǎhuǒjī	名	lighter
16	一齐	yìqí	副	at the same time; together
17	寿星	shòuxing	名	the one whose birthday is being celebrated

18 许愿	xǔ yuàn	动	make a wish
19 吹	chuī	动	blow; puff
20 灭	miè	动	(of a light, fire, etc.) go out
21 实现	shíxiàn	动	realize; come true
22 加劲儿	jiā jìnr	动	put more energy into
23 玩具	wánjù	名	toy
24 属于	shǔyú	动	belong to
25 属	shǔ	动	be born in the year of

三 注释 Notes

(一) 十二生肖

中国人用十二种动物来记人的出生年份。这十二种动物依次是：鼠、牛、虎、兔、龙、蛇、马、羊、猴、鸡、狗、猪，称为十二生肖。"属狗的"就是狗年出生的。

Chinese people use twelve animals to mark a person's birth year, i.e. rat, ox, tiger, rabbit, dragon, snake, horse, goat, monkey, rooster, dog and boar. The twelve animals are known as "Twelve Chinese Zodiac Signs". "属狗的" means the person was born in the year of dog.

（二）“把”字句与一般动词谓语句的主要区别

“把”字句中“把”的宾语大都是已知的信息，句子的语义焦点在动词的附带成分上。而一般动词谓语句的语义焦点是不清楚的：一般情况下，句子的语义焦点在宾语上；在一定的情况下，几乎每个成分都可以成为语义焦点。

In a “把” sentence, the object of “把” is usually the information already known, and the semantic focus of the sentence is on the incidental components of the verb. However, the semantic focus of a general verb predicate sentence is not clear. In general, the semantic focus of a sentence is on the object, while under certain circumstances, almost every component can become the semantic focus.

“把”字句：我把那条牛仔裤买回来了。

句中的“牛仔裤”是已知的旧信息。它什么样、多少钱等，是说话人和听话人都知道的。可能是他们昨天在商店里看过的那条，只是因为某种原因，昨天没有买。

“牛仔裤” in this sentence is the information already known. What it looked like or how much it cost was known to both the speaker and the listener. It could be the pair they saw in the store yesterday, but for some reason, they didn’t buy it.

一般动词谓语句：我买回来了一条牛仔裤。

句中的“牛仔裤”是新信息。它什么样、多少钱，是听话人不知道的。

“牛仔裤” in the sentence is new information. The listener doesn’t know what it looks like or how much it costs.

四 练习 Exercises

（一）朗读 Read aloud

1. 朗读下列发音相近的词语 Read aloud the following words with similar pronunciation

huā bù 花布	huàbù 画布	dìbǎn 地板	dìtǎn 地毯

xiǎnde 显得	xiándé 贤德	yìqí 一齐	yìqǐ 一起
xǔ yuàn 许愿	xìyuàn 戏院	shòuxing 寿星	qiúxīng 球星

2. 朗读下列短语 Read the following phrases aloud

祝：祝你生日快乐　祝你圣诞快乐　祝你新年快乐
祝你身体健康　祝爷爷奶奶健康长寿

铺：铺桌布　铺地毯　铺床　铺被子　铺开　铺上

显得：显得很干净　显得很精神　显得很年轻　显得很脏
显得很乱

蛋糕：做蛋糕　买蛋糕　切蛋糕　吃蛋糕

（二）替换并朗读 Replace and read aloud

1. 咱们把客厅布置布置吧。

房间　宿舍　教室
会场　会议室　礼堂

2. 先把这些乱七八糟的东西收拾一下。

书报杂志　衣服
屋子　桌子上的东西

3. 把那瓶花摆在桌子上吧。

教室里　客厅里
阳台上　窗台上

4. 这一收拾，客厅里显得又干净又整齐。

屋子里　教室里　房间里
宿舍　楼里

5. 祝你生日快乐！

爸爸　妈妈　爷爷
奶奶　姥姥　姥爷

6. 要说她是属<u>狗</u>的。

鼠	牛	虎	兔	龙	蛇
马	羊	猴	鸡	猪	

7. 把<u>灯</u>关上吧？

窗户	门	电视
火	手机	空调

8. A：昨晚的生日晚会怎么样？
   B：我们班大部分同学都参加了，大家<u>又说又笑</u>，可<u>热闹</u>了。

又唱又跳	高兴
又吃又喝	快乐
又喝又聊	开心

（三）**选词填空并朗读下列句子** Choose the appropriate words to fill in the blanks and read aloud the following sentences

给　铺　为　插　什么　一下

1. 今晚要在这儿________丹尼丝开生日晚会，咱们把客厅布置布置吧。
2. 先把这些乱七八糟的东西收拾________。
3. A：你看，把这两张桌子对在一起，摆在中间，把椅子放在四周，怎么样？
   B：行。这桌子上也太乱了，把这些画报、杂志放到________地方去呢？
4. 把不用的东西先收起来，再把桌子擦擦，把我这块儿花布________上吧。
5. 把我们买的那束鲜花________在花瓶里，放在桌子上吧。
6. 地板有点儿脏，你把墩布递________我，我再把地板拖一拖。

关 成 把 要是

1. 把蜡烛插在蛋糕上吧。应该插二十支，二十岁了嘛。好，请寿星________蜡烛点上吧。
2. A：把灯________上吧？
   B：关上吧。来，让我们祝丹尼丝生日快乐！
3. A：该吹蜡烛了。丹尼丝，你________一口气把蜡烛全吹灭，你许的愿就都能实现。
   B：真的吗？那我可得加把劲儿。
5. 请寿星来切蛋糕吧。把它切________二十块吧，我们一共二十个人。

参加 礼物 怎么 哪儿 所以

1. 昨天晚上你去________了？手机还关机了，我去找你，你不在。
2. 昨晚丹尼丝过生日，我去________她的生日晚会了。
3. 我们班大部分同学都去了。大家又说又笑，一起吃蛋糕、一起唱歌。因为是第一次在中国过生日，________她特别高兴。你看，这是我给她拍的照片。
4. A：真漂亮！她身边________那么多玩具小狗啊？
   B：这是同学们送给她的生日________，因为丹尼丝是属狗的。

（四）完成下列会话并大声朗读 Complete the following conversations and read them aloud

1. A：你的生日是几月几号？
   B：________________________________。
2. A：你是属什么的？
   B：________________________________。
3. A：今晚要在这儿举行生日晚会，咱们把客厅布置布置吧。
   B：________________________________。（怎么 一起）

4. A：桌子上太乱了，把这些画报、杂志放到什么地方去呢？
   B：________________________。（把　收）
5. A：地板有点儿脏，你把墩布递给我，我再把地板拖一拖。
   B：________________________。（累　休息　让）
6. A：蛋糕上插多少支蜡烛？
   B：________________________。
7. A：________________________？
   （把　蛋糕　切　多少）
   B：切成二十块吧，我们一共二十个人。
8. A：________________________？（怎么样）
   B：可热闹了。大部分同学们都来了，大家又说又笑，一起吃蛋糕、喝酒、唱歌，高兴极了。

（五）**完成下列句子并大声朗读** Complete the following sentences and read them aloud

1. 昨晚丹妮丝过生日，大家________________，非常开心。
   （一齐　唱）
2. 老师问，明天我们去爬山好不好，大家________________。
   （一齐）
3. 他俩________________四年，产生了感情，所以，一毕业就结婚了。
   （一起）
4. 我们俩不________________，她住校外中国人家里，我住校内留学生公寓。
   （一起）
5. 我看今天的上海，跟________________。（差不多）
6. 每课后边的诗词，我________________。（差不多　都）

（六）**和同学一起表演课文** Act out the text with your classmates

（七）**自由表达** Express yourself freely

介绍一次自己参加过的生日聚会或者谈谈自己过生日的计划：包括时间、地点、邀请哪些人、准备什么节目等。

（八）读后说 Read the passage and say it

1. 朗读 Read aloud

祝你生日快乐

我们班有 18 个同学，来自 13 个国家。第一天上课，老师就让班长把全班同学的姓名、国籍、手机号和生日都记了下来。为了交流信息、联络感情，全班还在微信上建了一个群。老师说，同学们来自五洲四海，能在一起学习很难得。今后我们班要像一个大家庭一样，大家要互相关心、互相爱护、互相学习、互相帮助。我们这 18 个同学，差不多每个月都有人过生日，以后不管谁过生日，大家都要为他举办一个生日晚会，使我们在中国的留学生活过得更加丰富多彩、更加愉快。

昨天是丹尼丝的生日，我们在教室为她举行了生日晚会，老师也参加了。同学们送给她了一些生日礼物，我送给她了一个玩具小狗，她很喜欢，我说："你是属狗的，我也是属狗的，我们同岁，祝你生日快乐！"

我们从饭店点了很多好吃的菜，有的同学还喝了啤酒和葡萄酒。我不会喝酒，只喝了两杯茶。

丹尼丝在蛋糕上插上了 20 支蜡烛。我们把蜡烛点上、把灯关上，在烛光中一起唱"祝你生日快乐"。丹尼丝一脸喜悦，高兴地把蜡烛吹灭。灯亮了，大家一阵欢呼，气氛非常热烈。丹尼丝把蛋糕切成了 20 块，每人 1 块，大家一边吃，一边聊。

吃完蛋糕，爱德华弹起了吉他，大家跟他一起唱了起来。我们唱了几支中文歌，还唱了各自国家的歌。丹尼丝说，谢谢大家给她过生日，她感到非常快乐。同学们说，我们也都很快乐。

小词典

国籍	guójí	名	nationality
交流	jiāoliú	动、名	interchange; exchange
联络	liánluò	动	contact

感情	gǎnqíng	名	friendly contacts
五洲四海	wǔzhōu-sìhǎi		whole world; all parts of the world
丰富多彩	fēngfù-duōcǎi		rich and varied
喜悦	xǐyuè	形	happy; cheerful
气氛	qìfēn	名	atmosphere
热烈	rèliè	形	lively; warm
吉他	jítā	名	guitar

2. 回答下列问题 Answer the following questions

（1）“我们”班有多少个学生？

（2）“我们”为什么要建微信群？

（3）昨天是谁的生日？“我们”是怎么为她过生日的？

（4）“我”送给了丹尼丝一件什么礼物？“我”为什么要送给她这么一件礼物？

（5）昨天的生日晚会怎么样？

3. 你是 A，请你向 B 提问 Supposing you are A, ask B questions

（1）A：______________________________？（多少　国家）

B：我们班的同学来自 13 个国家。

（2）A：______________________________？

（老师　班长　做什么）

B：老师要班长把全班同学的姓名、国籍、手机号和生日都记了下来，全班建了一个微信群。

（3）A：______________________________？

（怎么　为　过　生日）

B：每个同学过生日，我们都为他举行一个生日晚会。

（4）A：______________________________？（怎么样）

B：我们班就像一个大家庭一样，同学们互相关心、互相爱护、互相学习、互相帮助。在这个班学习，大家都感到非常快乐。

（5）A：______________________________？（给　谁）

B：昨天我们为丹尼丝举行了生日宴会。

（6）A：______________________________？（唱　什么）

B：我们唱了中文歌，还唱了各自国家的歌。

4. 复述这篇课文 Retell this text

（九）朗读中国经典诗词，请注意语音语调 Read aloud the classic Chinese poem and pay attention to the pronunciation and intonation

Shuǐ Diào Gē Tóu
水 调 歌 头

[Sòng] Sū Shì
［宋］苏 轼（1037—1101）

Míngyuè jǐshí yǒu? Bǎ jiǔ wèn qīngtiān.
明月 几时 有？把 酒 问 青天。
Bù zhī tiānshàng gōngquè, jīn xī shì hé nián.
不知 天上 宫阙，今 夕 是 何 年。
Wǒ yù chéng fēng guīqù, yòu kǒng qiónglóu-yùyǔ, gāochù bú shèng hán.
我 欲 乘 风 归去，又 恐 琼楼玉宇，高处 不 胜 寒。
Qǐ wǔ nòng qīng yǐng, hé sì zài rénjiān.
起 舞 弄 清 影，何 似 在 人间。

Zhuǎn zhū gé, dī qǐ hù, zhào wú mián.
转 朱阁，低 绮 户，照 无 眠。
Bù yīng yǒu hèn, hé shì cháng xiàng bié shí yuán?
不 应 有 恨，何 事 长 向 别 时 圆？
Rén yǒu bēihuān-líhé, yuè yǒu yīnqíng-yuánquē, cǐ shì gǔ nán quán.
人 有 悲欢离合，月 有 阴晴圆缺，此 事 古 难 全。
Dàn yuàn rén chángjiǔ, qiān lǐ gòng chánjuān.
但 愿 人 长久，千 里 共 婵娟。

（十）请欣赏下列著名的词句 Please enjoy the following famous saying

Qiān lǐ sòng émáo, lǐ qīng qíngyì zhòng.

千里送鹅毛，礼轻情意重。

A small gift from afar conveys deep feeling.

Dì-wǔshísì kè　Zánmen bāo dùn jiǎozi chī ba

第五十四课　咱们包顿饺子吃吧

Lesson 54　Let's make dumplings

一　课文 Text

（一）咱们包顿饺子吃吧

（星期天，玛丽和山本一起包饺子……）

玛丽：我在老师家学会了包饺子，今天咱们也包顿饺子吃吧。

山本：好啊。老师说，饺子好不好吃的关键是馅儿，馅儿好，饺子就好吃，你来做馅儿吧。

玛丽：好，我先把馅儿做好，你来把面和上吧。

（玛丽做馅儿，山本和面）

山本：你看这样可以吗？

玛丽：挺好的，不软也不硬。

山本：我来擀皮儿吧。先把面搓成面棍儿，再把它切成一小段一小段的，撒上一些面粉，把它们揉成面球，用手把它这么一摁，擀成圆形的面皮儿。你看这样行吗？

玛丽：很好。我把馅儿也做好了，开始包吧。我得看着老师给的说明书，把馅儿放在皮儿中间，用皮儿把馅儿包起来，再把两边捏上。这样，一个饺子就做成了。你看，像不像小老鼠？

山本：不管它像什么，反正是饺子，不是馒头。

（二）千万别把饺子放进冷水里煮

玛丽：（看说明书）好，现在可以煮了。先把水倒进锅里，注意，要等水开了才能把饺子放进去，千万别把饺子放进冷水里煮。

山本：是。如果把饺子放进冷水里的话，就会把饺子煮破，饺子一破就成片儿汤了。

玛丽：好了，水开了，可以把饺子放进去了。（看说明书）把饺子下到锅里以后，再用勺子轻轻地搅一搅，别让饺子粘在锅底。好，现在把锅盖儿盖上吧。

山本：水又开了，把锅盖儿拿下来，我来加一点儿冷水。

玛丽：我觉得煮得差不多了，你看，饺子都漂上来了。山本，你来尝尝，看熟了没有。

山本：（尝了一个）熟了，可以捞了。

玛丽：来，把饺子捞到这个盘子里。

山本：我已经把醋和蒜汁放在桌子上了，你想吃的话就自己来吧。

玛丽：（吃了一个）好吃，真好吃。

山本：我拿啤酒来，咱们来干一杯，庆贺我们包饺子成功。

玛丽：干杯！

山本：干杯！

二 生词 New Words

1	顿	dùn	量	*a measure word used to indicate frequency*
2	馅儿	xiànr	名	stuffing
3	和	huó	动	mix (flour) with water
4	软	ruǎn	形	soft
5	硬	yìng	形、副	hard
6	擀	gǎn	动	roll (dough, etc. with a rolling pin)
7	皮儿	pír	名	(dumpling) wrapper
8	搓	cuō	动	rub with the hands
9	棍儿	gùnr	名	stick; rod

10	段	duàn	量	section; part
11	撒	sǎ	动	sprinkle
12	面粉	miànfěn	名	flour
13	揉	róu	动	knead; roll
14	摁	èn	动	press
15	面皮儿	miànpír	名	wrapper (of dumplings, etc.)
16	边	biān	名	edge; margin
17	捏	niē	动	squeeze
18	老鼠	lǎoshǔ	名	mouse
19	反正	fǎnzhèng	副	*used to indicate the same result despite different circumstances*
20	煮	zhǔ	动	boil
21	锅	guō	名	pot
22	片儿汤	piànrtāng	名	flat pieces of dough served with soup
	汤	tāng	名	soup
23	开	kāi	动	boil
24	勺子	sháozi	名	spoon
25	搅	jiǎo	动	stir
26	粘	zhān	动	stain
27	底	dǐ	名	bottom
28	盖儿	gàir	名	lid; cover
29	盖	gài	动	put a cover (over...); cover
30	漂	piāo	动	float
31	熟	shú	形	make well-cooked

32 捞	lāo	动	scoop up (from liquid)
33 盘子	pánzi	名	plate
34 醋	cù	名	vinegar
35 蒜	suàn	名	garlic
36 成功	chénggōng	动、形	succeed; successful

三 注释 Notes

(一)“把”字句的功能

“把”字句常常用于描述一个动作及其结果，或对人发出某种指令。例如：

A “把” sentence is often used to describe an action and its result, or to give some kind of instruction to somebody. For example:

1. 我先把馅儿做好，你来把面和上吧。
2. 我来擀皮儿吧，先把面搓成面棍，再把它切成一小段一小段的，撒上一些面粉，把它们揉成面球，用手把它这么一摁，擀成圆形的面皮儿。你看这样行吗？
3. 把馅儿放在皮儿中间，用皮儿把馅儿包起来，再把两边捏住。这样，一个饺子就做成了。
4. 千万别把饺子放进冷水里煮。

(二) 反正

副词“反正”表示情况虽然不同，但是结果一样。常常和“不管、不论、无论”连用。例如：

The adverb “反正” means that the situation is different, but the result is the same. It is often used with “不管，不论，无论”. For example:

1. 不管他去不去，反正我一定去。

2. 不论你相信不相信，反正我信。

3. 无论广告怎么说，反正我不买。

四 练习 Exercises

（一）朗读 Read aloud

1. 朗读下列发音相近的词语 Read aloud the following words with similar pronunciation

xuézhe 学着	xuézhě 学者	zánmen 咱们	zànměi 赞美
huó miàn 和 面	huòmiǎn 豁免	miànfěn 面粉	miǎn fèi 免 费
fǎnzhèng 反正	fǎnyìng 反映	qìnghè 庆贺	qǐng hē 请 喝

2. 朗读下列短语 Read the following phrases aloud

包：包饺子　包包子　包粽子　包上了　包住了　包不住

反正：反正是饺子　反正我不去　反正我不相信　反正我不拍

煮：煮饺子　煮一煮　煮熟了　没煮熟

汤：片儿汤　鸡蛋汤　汤很好喝　汤有点儿淡

盖：盖盖子　盖被子　盖上吧　盖不上　盖不住

加：加点儿水　加点儿汤　加点儿糖　加点儿醋　加点儿牛奶

熟：饺子熟了　熟人　我跟他不熟　我们很熟

3. 朗读下列词组，注意“不”的声调 Read the following phrases and pay attention to the tone of “不”

不软也不硬　不热也不冷　不长也不短　不咸也不淡

不大也不小　不多也不少　不肥也不瘦　不前也不后

（二）替换并朗读 Replace and read aloud

1. 你把面和上吧。

大衣	穿
手机	带
蜡烛	插
眼镜	戴
要寄的快件	包
锅盖儿	盖

2. 把面搓成面棍儿。

面块	揉	面球
课文	翻译	汉语
会话	改	短文
故事	改	会话

3. 我把饺子捞到这个盘子里了。

醋和蒜汁	放在	桌子上
车	开到	楼门口
朋友	送到	机场
桌子	搬到	外边去
那盆花	放在	阳台上
这首诗	记在	心里

4. 饺子一破就成片儿汤了。

你	尝	知道熟不熟了
我	看说明书	知道怎么用了
我	到课堂	有点儿兴奋
我	说“把”字句	出错
我	读这篇课文	想笑

5. 饺子好不好吃的关键是馅儿，馅儿好，饺子就好吃。

这次留学能不能去成的	奖学金，奖学金多，留学就没有问题
汉语能不能学好的	听和说，听说过关了，就能学好
HSK 考试能不能通过的	读写，读写好，拿到证书就没问题

6. 你看我这么包对不对？

写	做	跳
装	说	翻译

7. 挺好的，不软不硬。

大	小	肥	瘦	冷	热
咸	淡	长	短	粗	细

8. 如果把饺子放进冷水里的话，就会把饺子煮破。

不经常复习学过的生词和句子	容易忘记
不预习	听不懂老师说的是什么
不经常听录音	不可能提高听力水平
不常跟中国人谈话	很难提高口语能力
不坚持天天上课	很难学好汉语

（三）**用“反正”完成下列句子并大声朗读** Complete the following sentences with “反正” and read them aloud

1. 不管学习上遇到多大的困难，__________________。（不怕）
2. 不管他怎么说，__________________。（答应）
3. 不管明天天气怎么样，__________________。（出发）
4. 无论你买不买，__________________。（买）
5. 不论他说什么，__________________。（同意）
6. 去不去你自己决定，__________________。（告诉）

（四）**选词填空并朗读下列句子** Choose the appropriate words to fill in the blanks and read aloud the following sentences

上　会　把　先　就　也

1. 我在老师家学________了包饺子，今天咱们也包顿饺子吃吧。
2. 饺子好不好吃的关键是馅儿，馅儿好，饺子________好吃。
3. 我________把馅儿做好，你来把面和上吧。
4. A：面和成这样可以吗？

   B：挺好的，不软________不硬。
5. 我来擀皮儿吧。先________一块面搓成面棍儿，再把它切成一小段一小段的，撒上一些面粉，把它们揉成面球，用手把它这么一摁，擀成圆形的面皮儿。
6. 我把饺子馅儿做好了，我们开始包吧。要把饺子馅儿放在饺子皮儿中间，用皮儿把馅儿包起来，再把两边捏________。这样，一个饺子就做成了。

粘　的话　到　差不多　别　把

1. 现在我们煮饺子。先把水倒进锅里，注意，要等水开了才能把饺子放进去，千万________把饺子放进冷水里煮。
2. 如果把饺子放进冷水里的话，就会________饺子煮破，饺子一破就成片儿汤了。
3. 把饺子下到锅里以后，再用勺子轻轻地搅一搅，别让饺子________在锅底。好，现在把锅盖儿盖上吧。
4. A：我觉得煮得________了，你看，饺子都漂上来了。你来尝尝，看熟了没有。

   B：熟了，可以捞了。
5. 来，你把饺子捞________这个盘子里。
6. 我已经把醋和蒜汁放在桌子上了，你想吃________就自己来吧。

摁　反正　开　揉　勺子　熟

1. 肚子不舒服的时候，你可以自己________一________。中医认为，坚持每天揉揉肚子，对身体很有好处。
2. 身上有肌肉僵硬（jiāngyìng, stiff）的地方，用手________一________，就会舒服一些。
3. 不管你相信不相信，________我相信按摩和针灸是能治病的。因为我的腰疼就是大夫给我扎针扎好的。
4. 我到现在也不明白，中国人为什么那么爱喝________水。我们从小到大都是喝冷水。
5. 其实，中国人吃饭除了用筷子，也用________。喝汤总不能用筷子吧。
6. 饺子有生________，人也有生________。汉语说“熟人好办事儿”，你知道是什么意思吗？

（五）完成下列会话并大声朗读 Complete the following conversations and read them aloud

1. A：玛丽和山本要做什么？
   B：________________________________。
2. A：饺子好不好吃的关键是什么？
   B：________________________________。
3. A：谁和的面？面和得怎么样？
   B：________________________________。
4. A：山本是怎么擀饺子皮儿的？
   B：________________________________。
5. A：玛丽是怎么包饺子的？
   B：________________________________。
6. A：为什么不能把饺子放进冷水里煮？
   B：________________________________。

7. A：把饺子下到锅里后，为什么要搅一搅？

B：________________________________。

8. A：她们第一次做的饺子怎么样？

B：________________________________。

（六）**和同学一起表演课文** Act out the text with your classmates

（七）**自由表达** Express yourself freely

和同学一起包一顿饺子，用汉语说说你们是怎么包的。（请尽可能地用上“把”字句）

（八）**读后说** Read the passage and say it

1. 朗读 Read aloud

包饺子练习“把”字句

那天老师跟我们一起包饺子、吃饺子，吃完饺子，大家都不愿意离开。老师就说，那咱们就聊天儿吧。老师让我们大家说说自己来中国以后的生活，并且希望我们最好能用上“把”字句。

原来，老师不只是让我们包饺子、吃饺子，还想通过包饺子，让我们懂得“把”字句的用法。

“把”字句对我们这些学汉语的外国人来说，是一个很难的句型。我在日常生活中也学着用“把”字句，但常常一用就错，所以不太敢用“把”字句。

老师对我们说，世界上最可原谅的错误可能就是说外语的时候说错了。老师还说，她也学过外语，她说错的句子可能比我们多得多。所以，学习汉语不怕说错，就怕不说。不说，当然不会出错，但也永远都不会说。在课堂上要大胆地说，说错了，老师会帮助我们。在别的中国人面前，也要勇敢地说，大多数中国人一定会帮助我们。只要多说多练，一定能说一口标准流利的汉语普通话。

来中国快一年了，我越来越喜欢学汉语了。

小词典

用法	yòngfǎ	名	usage
句型	jùxíng	名	sentence pattern
日常	rìcháng	形	daily; everyday
敢	gǎn	动	dare
原谅	yuánliàng	动	forgive
也许	yěxǔ	副	maybe
大胆	dàdǎn	形	bold; brave
勇敢	yǒnggǎn	形	brave
标准	biāozhǔn	名、形	standard; standardized

2. 回答下列问题 Answer the following questions

（1）那天老师跟“我们”一起做什么了？

（2）老师想跟“我们”练习什么句型？

（3）你在日常生活中敢用“把”字句吗？

（4）你愿意跟中国人用汉语谈话吗？

（5）你怕说错汉语吗？

（6）你是不是越来越喜欢学汉语了？

3. 你是 A，请你向 B 提问 Supposing you are A, ask B questions

（1）A：____________________？（什么）

B：老师和我们一起包饺子。

（2）A：____________________？（为什么）

B：老师想让我们一边包饺子，一边练习说“把”字句。

（3）A：____________________？（什么）

B：我们一起聊天儿，说自己来中国以后的生活。

（4）A：____________________？（怎么　鼓励）

B：她说，说汉语说错了没关系。

（5）A：________________________________？

B：她还说谁都有学习外语时说错的经历。

（6）A：________________________________？

B：我越来越喜欢学习汉语了。

（九）朗读中国经典诗词，请注意语音语调 Read aloud the classic Chinese poem and pay attention to the pronunciation and intonation

Zèng Liú Jǐngwén
赠 刘 景文

[Sòng] Sū Shì
［宋］苏 轼（1037—1101）

Hé jìn yǐ wú qíng yǔ gài, jú cán yóu yǒu ào shuāng zhī.
荷尽已无擎雨盖，菊残犹有傲霜枝。
Yì nián hǎojǐng jūn xū jì, zhèng shì chéng huáng jú lǜ shí.
一年好景君须记，正是橙黄橘绿时。

（十）请欣赏下列著名的词句 Please enjoy the following famous saying

Mǐn ér hàoxué, bù chǐ xià wèn.
敏而好学，不耻下问。

Quick-minded and eager to learn, he is never ashamed to consult his inferiors.

Dì-wǔshíwǔ kè　Wǒ jiù xiǎng ānān-jìngjìng de dú shū

第五十五课　我就想安安静静地读书

Lesson 55　I just want to read quietly

一　课文 Text

（两个日本留学生在交谈）

松山：昨天晚上的电视你看了吗？

村上：什么电视？

松山：世界杯足球决赛呀。

村上：没看，我不看电视。

松山：你不看电视！那你看什么？

村上：看书。

松山：看什么书？

村上：什么书都看，日本的、中国的，东方的、西方的，现代的、古代的。

松山：你是上网看吗？

村上：我不上网。

松山：那你怎么知道国内外新闻哪？

村上：我不想知道那些，我就想安安静静地读书。

松山：你看得懂中文书吗？

村上：我现在看的都是翻译成日文的译本。就是为了能看懂中文原文，我才来中国留学的。

松山：是这样啊。

村上：从我懂事起，爷爷就给我讲中国，讲中国历史，这让我对中国古代的圣贤非常敬慕，也让我对中国文化产生了浓厚的兴趣。所以，我想在大学四年内，专心致志，闭门读书。

松山：你要研究中国历史吗？

村上：研究现在还谈不上。

松山：那你是想学音乐家团伊玖磨先生吗？

村上：是的，我要向先生学习。

松山：他太怪了！一个人在太平洋的一个小岛上一住就是几十年，没有电视，没有收音机，拒绝各种社会信息，实在让人太难理解了。

村上：其实，他一年只在岛上住九个月，其他时间都周游世界去了。先生的人生丰富多彩，光中国他就来过六十多次，最后还是在中国去世的。

松山：作为杰出的音乐家，他在日本无人不知啊！

村上：关于先生的事儿，我想中国音乐人也都知道吧。因为他为日中文化交流做出了巨大的贡献。

松山：因此，你也想像他那样吗？

村上：我现在只是想多读点儿书，至于今后做什么，怎么生活，我想书会告诉我。

松山：你这样，不觉得寂寞吗？

村上：不。对我来说，每天有书读是一种享受。

松山：是吗？村上，我不太赞成你这样做，但我尊重你的选择。能不能加你的微信啊？

村上：对不起，我没有微信。

松山：啊！

二 生词 New Words

1	决赛	juésài	动	play in the final
2	新闻	xīnwén	名	news
3	翻译	fānyì	动	translate
4	译本	yìběn	名	translation
5	原文	yuánwén	名	the original
6	懂事	dǒng shì	形	sensible
7	历史	lìshǐ	名	history
8	圣贤	shèngxián	名	sage; saint
9	敬慕	jìngmù	动	worship
10	浓厚	nónghòu	形	strong; deep
11	专心致志	zhuānxīn-zhìzhì		be absorbed (in); absorbedly
12	闭	bì	动	close; shut
13	研究	yánjiū	动	research; study
14	谈不上	tánbushàng		far from; be out of the question
15	先生	xiānsheng	名	Mr.
16	怪	guài	形、副	strange; odd; strangely; oddly
17	岛	dǎo	名	island
18	收音机	shōuyīnjī	名	radio
19	理解	lǐjiě	动	comprehend; understand
20	其他	qítā	代	other
21	周游	zhōuyóu	动	travel round
22	去世	qùshì	动	die; pass away
23	作为	zuòwéi	介	as

24	杰出	jiéchū	形	outstanding
25	无人不知	wúrén-bùzhī		to a proverb; known to all
26	关于	guānyú	介	about; with regard to
27	巨大	jùdà	形	enormous; tremendous
28	贡献	gòngxiàn	动、名	contribute; contribution
29	因此	yīncǐ	连	therefore; hence
30	至于	zhìyú	动、介	go as far as to; as for; as to
31	赞成	zànchéng	动	approve of; agree with
32	尊重	zūnzhòng	动	esteem; respect

专名 Zhuānmíng Proper Nouns

1	村上	Cūnshàng	name of a person
2	世界杯	Shìjièbēi	World Cup
3	东方	Dōngfāng	the East
4	西方	Xīfāng	the West
5	太平洋	Tàipíng Yáng	Pacific Ocean

三 注释 Notes

(一) 团伊玖磨 Tuányī Jiǔmó (Dan Ikuma, 1924-2001)

团伊玖磨先生是日本著名的作曲家。他深受中国传统文化的影响，一生致力于日中两国之间的文化交流，曾当过日中文化交流协会会长。除了作曲，先生还以写作散文著称于世。他在《朝日画报》上的专栏《烟斗之烟》(一作《烟斗随笔》)，一写就是 36 年。他是日本家喻户晓的人物。

Dan Ikuma is a famous Japanese composer who is also deeply influenced by Chinese history and culture. He devoted all his life to cultural exchange between China and Japan, and was the President of Sino-Japanese Cultural Exchange Association. Besides composing, he is also famous for his proses. His column "Pipe Smoke" (aka "Pipe Essay") in the *Asahi Graph* has been written for 36 year. In Japan, he is a house-hold name.

（**提示**：如果你要了解团伊玖磨先生更多的信息，请问问百度或谷歌。）

（二）从……起

"从……起"可以表示时间也可以表示处所、来源。例如：

"从……起" is used to indicate either the time or the place/origin. For example:

1. 从我上高中起，就想着将来要出国留学。
2. 我大学期间，利用寒暑假，从北京起，几乎走遍了大半个中国。

（三）无……不……

"无……不……"是个双重否定格式，表示十分肯定。例如：

"无……不……" is a double negative format, meaning "very sure". For example:

无人不知：没有人不知道＝都知道

无所不至：没有达不到的地方＝什么地方都到得了

无往不胜：到什么地方没有不胜的＝都能胜利

无微不至：没有一个小地方没有想到的＝都想到了

（四）一……就是……

"一……就是……"表示一个动作或情况延续的时间比较长。例如：

"一……就是……" indicates that an action or a situation lasts for a long time. For example:

1. 他喜欢玩儿手机游戏，一玩儿就是一个多钟头。
2. 姐姐去中国留学，一去就是四年。

（五）至于

常用在第二个分句前，表示提起另外一件事。例如：

It is often used before the second clause, indicating to mention another thing. For example:

1. 我知道他回国了，至于什么时候走的，我就不清楚了。
2. 我现在听说还可以，至于读和写，还是比较困难的。
3. 我想先把汉语学好，至于将来做什么，以后再说。

四 练习 Exercises

（一）朗读 Read aloud

1. 朗读下列发音相近的词语 Read aloud the following words with similar pronunciation

ānjìng 安静	gānjìng 干净	dú shū 读书	dúchǔ 独处
juésài 决赛	juésè 角色	lǐjiě 理解	lǐjié 礼节
dǒng shì 懂事	tóngshí 同时	lìshǐ 历史	lǐshì 理事

2. 朗读下列短语 Read the following phrases and sentences aloud

安静：这里很安静　安静的环境　安安静静地读书

敬慕：很敬慕他　敬慕古代的圣贤　敬慕他的人品

家：音乐家　科学家　文学家　哲学家　画家　作家　书法家

杰出：杰出的音乐家　杰出的科学家　杰出的政治家　杰出的诗人

理解：非常理解　很难理解　理解不了　很理解你的想法

（二）替换并朗读 Replace and read aloud

1. 就是为了能<u>看懂中文原文</u>，我才来中国留学的。

看懂中文书
了解中国
吃好吃的中国菜
游山玩水
毕业后能找个好工作

2. 作为杰出的音乐家，他在日本无人不知呀！

诗人	中国
画家	意大利
科学家	全世界
政治家	欧洲
建筑师	法国
指挥家	音乐界

（三）**选词填空并朗读下列句子** Choose the appropriate words to fill in the blanks and read aloud the following sentences

才　都　门　什么　给　怎么

1. A：昨天晚上的电视你看了吗？
   B：我不看电视。
   A：你不看电视！那你看________？
   B：我看书，什么书________看，日本的、中国的，东方的、西方的，古代的、现代的。
2. A：那你________知道国内外新闻哪？
   B：我不想知道那些，我就想安安静静地读书。
3. A：你看得懂中文书吗？
   B：我现在看的都是翻译成日文的译本。就是想看懂中文，我________来中国留学的。
4. 从我懂事起，爷爷就________我讲中国，讲中国历史，这让我对中国古代的圣贤非常敬慕，也让我对中国文化产生了浓厚的兴趣。
5. 我想在大学这四年间，专心致志，闭________读书。

去世　知　理解　为　但　会

1. 这个先生也太怪了！一个人在太平洋的一个小岛上一住就是几十

年，没有电视，没有收音机，拒绝各种社会信息，实在让人太难________了。

2. 其实，他一年只在岛上住九个月，其他时间都周游世界去了。先生一生来中国六十多次，最后还是在中国________的。
3. 作为一位杰出的音乐家，他在日本无人不________呀！
4. 中国音乐人也都知道先生吧，他________日中文化交流做出了巨大的贡献。
5. 我现在只是想多读点儿书，至于今后做什么、怎么生活，我想书________告诉我。
6. A：村上，我不太赞成你这样做，________我尊重你的选择。能不能加你的微信哪？

   B：对不起，我没有微信。

浓厚　决赛　专心致志　拒绝　谈不上　怪

1. 世界杯________的那场球踢得十分精彩（jīngcǎi, wonderful）。
2. 我对中国古代的历史有着________的兴趣。
3. 要想研究什么问题，一定得________，不然是不会成功的。
4. 我只是对这个问题感兴趣，研究还________。
5. 历史上那些非常优秀的人，好像都有点儿________。
6. 先生在世时，一些电视台或报纸要采访（cǎifǎng, interview）他，他都________了。

贡献　至于　尊重　光　理解　周游

1. 世界各国都有自己的文化和文明，不同的文化和文明，应该互相________、互相学习。
2. 我学习外语的一个目的就是想________世界。
3. 学习汉语，________练习听说是不行的，一定要在提高听说能力的同时，使自己的读写能力也得到提高。

4. 她为世界和平做出了巨大的________，所以才获得了诺贝尔和平奖。

5. 我现在最想做的事儿，是先把汉语学好，________能不能实现自己的理想，还很难说。

6. 生活中，要被别人________是很难的。

（四）用“就是”完成下列句子并大声朗读 Complete the following sentences with “就是” and read them aloud

1. 他在电脑前一坐________________，常常忘了吃饭。
2. 他来中国一住________________，中国已经成了他的第二故乡。
3. 这次出国一去________________，不想家是不可能的。
4. 她汉语说得真好，一说________________，真让我羡慕。
5. 我这把吉他买回来以后，一放________________，从来没有弹过。
6. 爸爸热爱他的工作，一干________________。

（五）将 A、B 两列连线，组成一个句子，然后朗读 Match A with B to make correct sentences and read aloud

1.

A	B
中国人都知道先生吧，	他是世界知名的球星。
环保人士都知道他吧，	因为他演的电影在中国很红。
学书法的都知道他吧，	他在中国西部多年，种了很多树。
喜欢音乐的都知道他吧，	他为发展中美关系（guānxì, relationship）做出了巨大的贡献。
球迷们都喜欢他吧，	他的书法被称作天下第一行书（xíngshū, running script）。
很多年轻人是他的粉丝，	他是世界有名的音乐家。

2. A B

A	B
我现在只是想多读点儿书，	至于结不结婚，现在说太早。
我现在只是想学好汉语，	至于能不能当汉语老师，还很难说。
我现在只是想出国留学，	至于考不考 HSK，现在不好说。
我现在只是想好好谈恋爱，	至于工作的事儿，以后再说。
我现在只是想先好好学习，	至于以后做什么，回国再说
我现在才刚刚学习汉语，	至于以后做什么，书会告诉我的。

（六）**回答课文的问题** Answer the questions about the text

1. 你知道不知道日本的作曲家团伊玖磨？
2. 他一个人在太平洋的一个小岛上住了多少年？
3. 你能理解他这种生活吗？
4. 他在日本很有名，只是因为他是作曲家吗？

（七）**和同学一起表演课文** Act out the text with your classmates

（八）**自由表达** Express yourself freely

说说你对村上同学的看法，你能理解他吗？为什么？

（九）**读后说** Read the passage and say it

1. 朗读 Read aloud

音容永在

团伊玖磨是日本著名的作曲家。他的音乐作品在日本多次得奖，享有很高的声誉。他创作的歌剧《夕鹤》曾在中国演出，并获得了巨大成功。

自 1966 年起，团伊玖磨先后来中国访问或演出六十多次，为中日文化交流做出了很大的贡献。

在中国音乐界，团伊玖磨先生有着深远的影响。他曾经是中国音乐学院和上海音乐学院的客座教授，指挥过中国交响乐团等多家著名乐团。

除了作曲以外，团伊玖磨先生还是一位作家。他在杂志上开专栏写文章，每周一篇，连载长达36年。他的文字平实、幽默，很受读者欢迎。他在最后一篇文章中说：“再见了！我不会再回到这里了。老人是要离开的……”

谁也没想到，2001年5月17日，他在来中国苏州访问时突然病逝。

先生走了，但他谦和的笑容永远留在了人们心中。他美妙的音乐和文章也永远留在人世，滋润着人们的心灵。

小词典

音容	yīnróng	名	voice and look (of sb.)
永（远）	yǒng (yuǎn)	副	always; forever
作曲家	zuòqǔjiā	名	composer
得奖	dé jiǎng		win a prize
享有	xiǎngyǒu	动	enjoy
声誉	shēngyù	名	reputation
创作	chuàngzuò	动、名	compose; composition
歌剧	gējù	名	opera
曾经	céngjīng	副	once; ever
客座	kèzuò	形	visiting
指挥	zhǐhuī	动、名	conduct; conductor
交响乐	jiāoxiǎngyuè	名	symphony
乐团	yuètuán	名	philharmonic society
专栏	zhuānlán	名	special column
连载	liánzǎi	动	serialize
平实	píngshí	形	plain; simple and unadorned
病逝	bìngshì	动	die of an illness
谦和	qiānhé	形	modest and gentle

笑容	xiàoróng	名	smile
美妙	měimiào	形	wonderful; beautiful; splendid
滋润	zīrùn	动	nurture
心灵	xīnlíng	名	heart; soul

专名

夕鹤	Xī Hè	*Crane in the Evening*

2. 回答下列问题 Answer the following questions

（1）团伊玖磨先生是什么人？

（2）他与中国的关系怎么样？

（3）先生来过中国多少次？

（4）除了作曲以外，先生还做什么工作？

（5）先生是在哪儿去世的？

（6）先生把什么留在了世间？

3. 你是 A，请你向 B 提问 Supposing you are A, ask B questions

（1）A：________________？（什么　人）

B：团伊玖磨是日本著名作曲家。

（2）A：________________？

B：他的音乐作品在日本多次得奖，享有很高的声誉。

（3）A：________________？（多少）

B：自 1966 年起，团伊玖磨先后来中国访问或演出六十多次，为中日文化交流做出了很大的贡献。

（4）A：________________？

B：在中国音乐界，团伊玖磨先生有着深远的影响，他曾经是中国音乐学院和上海音乐学院的客座教授，指挥过中国交响乐团等多家著名乐团。

（5）A：________________________？（为什么）

B：除了作曲以外，团伊玖磨先生还是一位作家，他在杂志上开专栏写文章，每周一篇，连载长达36年。他的文字平实、幽默，很受读者欢迎。

（6）A：________________________？（留）

B：先生走了，但他谦和的笑容永远留在了人们心中，他美妙的音乐和文章也永远留在人世，滋润着人们的心灵。

（十）朗读中国经典诗词，请注意语音语调 Read aloud the classic Chinese poem and pay attention to the pronunciation and intonation

Jiāngnán Féng Lǐ Guīnián
江南 逢李龟年

[Táng] Dù Fǔ
[唐] 杜甫（712—770）

Qíwáng zhái lǐ xúncháng jiàn, Cuījiǔ táng qián jǐ dù wén.
岐王宅里寻常见，崔九堂前几度闻。
Zhèng shì Jiāngnán hǎo fēngjǐng, luò huā shíjié yòu féng jūn.
正是江南好风景，落花时节又逢君。

（十一）请欣赏下列著名的词句 Please enjoy the following famous saying

Zhīrénzhě zhì, zìzhīzhě míng.
知人者智，自知者明。

One who knows others is wise, one who knows himself is intelligent.

Dì-wǔshíliù kè Wǒ zhēn pèifú nǐ

第五十六课 我真佩服你

Lesson 56 I really admire you

一 课文 Text

（两个留学生在交谈）

A：你喜欢什么运动？

B：我喜欢滑冰、滑雪、游泳，还有乒乓球。

A：你游泳游得怎么样？

B：马马虎虎吧。我虽然喜欢运动，但水平都很一般。你擅长什么运动？

A：网球和高尔夫球。

B：是吗？这可是高级运动。你打得怎么样？

A：我参加过全国网球比赛，可惜后来因为手腕儿受伤，没能参加决赛。要不，说不定能得奖呢。

B：这么说，你当过网球运动员啊？

A：是啊，就是因为手腕儿受伤了，才不得不退役的。后来我爸爸建议我学外语，我就选择了汉语，来中国留学了。

B：是不是还念念不忘你的网球？

A：偶尔会。不过，现在我觉得学习一门外语也不错。特别是学了汉语以后，越学越觉得有意思，好像又找回了当运动员时的感觉。

B：我真佩服你，干什么都有那么一股争强好胜的劲头儿。

A：这可能是我当运动员时培养锻炼出来的吧。当运动员的，谁不争强好胜，谁不想当冠军呢？

B：我真应该好好向你学习。

A：哪里，你比我学得好啊。

二 生词 New Words

1	滑冰	huá bīng	动	skate
	滑雪	huá xuě	动	ski
	滑	huá	动、形	slip; slippery
2	马马虎虎	mǎmǎhūhū	形	not very good; so-so; not so bad
3	一般	yìbān	形	general; so-so
4	擅长	shàncháng	动	be good at; be expert in
5	高尔夫球	gāo'ěrfūqiú	名	golf
6	高级	gāojí	形	high-grade; high-level
7	全国	quánguó	名	whole nation (or country)
8	可惜	kěxī	形	regrettable
9	手腕儿	shǒuwànr	名	wrist
10	运动员	yùndòngyuán	名	sportsman or sportswoman
11	不得不	bùdébù		cannot but; have to
12	退役	tuì yì	动	retire
13	念念不忘	niànniàn-búwàng		constantly bear in mind; always keep in mind
	忘	wàng	动	forget
14	偶尔	ǒu'ěr	副	now and then; sometimes
15	门	mén	量	*a measure word for fields of study or technical training*
16	股	gǔ	量	*a measure word for gas, smell or strength*
17	争强好胜	zhēngqiáng-hàoshèng		aggressive; pushy
18	劲头儿	jìntóur	名	vigor; spirit

三 注释 Notes

（一）偶尔

副词“偶尔”表示有时候，发生的次数很少。例如：

The adverb “偶尔” means “sometimes”, indicating that something rarely happens. For example:

1. A：是不是还念念不忘你的网球？
   B：偶尔会。
2. 他晚上常常学习到很晚，只是偶尔看看电视新闻。
3. 我很少运动，偶尔去游游泳。
4. 院子里很安静，偶尔有几声鸟叫。

（二）谁不……

这是用疑问代词“谁”组成的反问句。汉语反问句的功能是表示强烈肯定或否定的语气，不要求回答。用肯定句反问，句子的意思是否定；用否定句反问，句子的意思是肯定。“谁不……”的意思是“谁都……”。例如：

This is a rhetorical question using the interrogative pronoun “谁”. The function of a Chinese rhetorical question is to express a strong affirmative or negative tone without requiring an answer. If it uses an affirmative sentence to ask a question, the meaning of the sentence is negative, and vice versa. “谁不……” means “谁都……”. For example:

1. 当运动员的，谁不争强好胜，谁不想当冠军呢？
   （谁都争强好胜，谁都想当冠军）
2. 这些孩子谁不想出去玩儿呀。（谁都想去玩儿）
3. 这么好的姑娘，谁不喜欢啊。（谁都喜欢她）

四 练习 Exercises

（一）朗读 Read aloud

1. 朗读下列发音相近的词语 Read aloud the following words with similar pronunciation

pèi fú 佩服	bēifù 背负	wǎngqiú 网 球	wǎnqiū 晚秋
kěxī 可惜	kěxǐ 可喜	tuìchū 退出	tuīchū 推出
zhēng qiáng 争 强	zhēngqiǎng 争抢	hào shèng 好 胜	háoshēng 毫升

2. 朗读下列短语 Read the following phrases aloud

擅长：擅长游泳　擅长书法　擅长画画儿　擅长打网球
高级：高级运动　高级水平　高级饭店　高级中学
全国：全国比赛　全国人民　全国高校　走遍全国
决赛：参加决赛　进入决赛　退出决赛　决赛资格
选择：选择专业　选择学校　选择工作　选择导师
念念不忘：对这件事儿念念不忘　对他 / 她念念不忘
念念不忘父母的恩情
偶尔：偶尔看看　偶尔玩儿玩儿　偶尔见个面　偶尔会想回国
好像：好像懂了　好像亲姐妹　好像在哪儿见过
好像回到了家乡

（二）替换并朗读 Replace and read aloud

1. A：你擅长什么？
   B：我擅长<u>游泳</u>。

书法	写作	弹琵琶
唱歌	跳舞	画画儿

2. A：你<u>游泳</u> <u>游</u>得怎么样？
   B：马马虎虎吧。

跳舞	跳	唱歌	唱
二胡	拉	琵琶	弹
汉语	说	画儿	画

3. 这么说，你当过网球运动员啊？

乐队指挥　网球教练
音乐老师　汉语翻译

4. A：是不是还念念不忘你的网球？
B：偶尔会。

你的足球　你住过的家
你以前的同学 / 朋友
那次失败的比赛　那次得奖

5. 我好像又找回了当运动员时的感觉。

当学生的　当年的那种
回到自己家里的　当冠军的

6. 我真佩服你，干什么都有那么一股争强好胜的劲头儿。

不怕失败　永远乐观
不达目的誓不罢休（shìbúbàxiū, never give up）
不服输（fúshū, indomitable）

（三）**选词填空并朗读下列句子** Choose the appropriate words to fill in the blanks and read aloud the following sentences

得　当　出来　向　回　但

1. 我虽然喜欢运动，________水平都很一般。
2. 我参加过全国网球比赛，可惜后来因为手腕儿受伤，没能参加决赛。要不，说不定能________奖呢。
3. A：这么说，你________过网球运动员啊？
   B：是呀，就是因为手腕儿受伤了，才不得不退役的。后来我爸爸建议我学外语，我就选择了汉语，来中国留学了。

4. A：是不是还念念不忘你的网球？
   B：偶尔会。不过，现在我觉得学习一门外语也不错。特别是学了汉语以后，越学越觉得有意思，好像又找________了当运动员时的感觉。
5. A：我真佩服你，干什么都有那么一股争强好胜的劲头儿。
   B：这可能是我当运动员时培养锻炼________的吧。
6. A：我真应该好好________你学习。
   B：哪里，你比我学得好啊。

念念不忘　争强好胜　高级　偶尔　可惜　要不

1. 我的计划是四年后通过 HSK________考试。
2. 昨天晚上的足球比赛非常精彩，________你没看。
3. 你还是给他打个电话吧，告诉他你不去了，________他得一直等着。
4. 我喜欢画画儿，这些都是我的作品，________拿出来看看，很有意思。
5. ________的性格有优点，也有缺点。我认为还是应该根据自己的实际情况，确定自己的人生目标比较好，不跟别人比，跟自己比。
6. 过去的事情该忘掉的一定要忘掉，如果总是________，对身体和精神都不好。

（四）用“不得不”完成下列句子并大声朗读 Complete the following sentences with “不得不” and read them aloud

1. 因为太晚了，没有公交车了，我们____________________。
2. 她坚持要我跟她一起去，____________________。
3. 我不想打针，可是大夫说，打针好得快，____________________。
4. 我在公园门口等了半天她也没来，____________________。
5. 她病了，而且病得很重，所以____________________。
6. 我的手机太旧了，不好用了，____________________。

（五）**完成下列会话并大声朗读** Complete the following conversations and read them aloud

1. A：你喜欢什么运动？

   B：________________________________。

2. A：你游泳游得怎么样？

   B：________________________________。

3. A：你从什么时候开始学习游泳的？

   B：________________________________。

4. A：你参加过比赛吗？

   B：________________________________。

5. A：这么说，你当过游泳运动员啊？

   B：________________________________。

6. A：你为什么要来中国留学？

   B：________________________________。

（六）**和同学一起表演课文** Act out the text with your classmates

（七）**自由表达** Express yourself freely

和一两个同学一起，互相说说自己佩服的人（同学、朋友、父母、明星等）：他 / 她是什么人？你为什么佩服他 / 她？

（八）**读后说** Read the passage and say it

1. 朗读 Read aloud

圆　梦

很早以前，我就有一个梦。那就是能到中国看看，看看举世闻名的长城，看看可爱的大熊猫，尝尝中国菜。

高中毕业时，当爸爸妈妈问我打算选哪个专业、考什么学校，我毫不犹豫地回答，我要学习汉语。经过努力，我顺利地考上了国内大学的中文系。可美中不足的是，在国内学习汉语，教师差不多都是本国人。

我们学校只有一位中国老师，而他一周只上三次课，同学们在一起也很少说汉语。所以我认为，国内大学没有良好的语言环境，要学好汉语是比较困难的。于是，我暗暗下决心，一定要找机会到中国留学。

一天，妈妈突然问我："你想不想出国留学？"说着，她把一张报纸递给了我。我看到上面有一个通知。通知说，凡是大学一、二年级的学生均可报名参加政府奖学金考试，前十名的学生就有机会公费到中国留学。

看到这个消息，我高兴极了！我想，机会来了，于是决心去试试。第二天我就报了名。我的学习成绩一直不错，所以我觉得考前十名没有太大问题。于是，我认真地做着准备。不过，考试那天我还是有点儿紧张，毕竟是第一次参加这样的考试。

一考完，我就盼着公布成绩，有时还担心自己考不上。没想到，成绩出来，我考了第三名！全家人都为我感到高兴，妈妈还流下了激动的眼泪。那时候我感觉我是世界上最幸福的人，我就要圆我的留学梦了。

去年九月我来到了向往已久的中国，开始了自己的留学生活。

一切都是那么美好，一切都让我感到新鲜有趣。我在这里认识了很多朋友，我们常常一起玩儿、一起学习。我对汉语学习的热情越来越高，对中国的历史文化和风俗习惯也越来越感兴趣。业余时间，我学书法，学二胡，学打太极拳，还学做中国菜。大家知道，中国菜品种丰富而且很好吃。做中国菜简直是一门艺术，有的菜做出来像画儿一样漂亮，我只想欣赏它的美，而不忍心吃掉它。

我觉得自己选择汉语专业非常明智，能来中国留学非常幸运。随着中国的不断发展和进步，学习汉语的人前途将更加光明远大。所以，我对未来充满了信心。将来我可能当翻译，也可能当一个汉语教师。无论干什么，我都会成为连接我们国家和中国友谊的桥梁。

小词典

圆梦	yuán mèng	动	make one's dream come true
举世闻名	jǔshì-wénmíng		world-famous

毫不犹豫	háo bù yóuyù		without the least hesitation
美中不足	měizhōng-bùzú		fly in the ointment
暗暗	àn'àn	副	secretly; inwardly; to oneself
均	jūn	副	all; without exception
政府	zhèngfǔ	名	government
奖学金	jiǎngxuéjīn	名	scholarship
公费	gōngfèi	名	funded by the state or the collective
公布	gōngbù	动	make public
向往	xiàngwǎng	动	yearn for
风俗	fēngsú	名	custom
明智	míngzhì	形	sensible; wise
随着	suízhe	介	(along) with
前途	qiántú	名	future; prospect
未来	wèilái	名	future
桥梁	qiáoliáng	名	bridge

2. 朗读下列问句并回答 Read aloud the interrogative sentences and answer the questions

(1)"圆梦"是什么意思？

(2)"我"很早以前有一个什么梦？

(3)"我"高中毕业时决定考什么专业？

(4)"我"为什么暗暗下决心要到中国留学？

(5)"我"是怎么取得公费留学资格的？

(6)"我"现在的感觉怎么样？

(7)"我"业余时间还学习什么？

(8)"我"为什么觉得自己的选择是明智的？

3. 你是 A，请你向 B 提问 Supposing you are A, ask B questions

（1）A：＿＿＿＿＿＿＿＿＿＿＿＿＿＿＿＿＿＿？（你　什么）

B：很早以前，我就有一个梦。那就是能到中国看看，看看举世闻名的长城，看看可爱的大熊猫，尝尝中国菜。

（2）A：＿＿＿＿＿＿＿＿＿＿＿＿＿＿＿＿＿＿？（什么）

B：高中毕业时，当爸爸妈妈问我打算选哪个专业、考什么学校，我毫不犹豫地回答，我要学习汉语。

（3）A：＿＿＿＿＿＿＿＿＿＿＿＿＿＿＿＿＿＿？（为什么）

B：因为我觉得在国内大学没有良好的语言环境，要学好汉语是比较困难的。于是，我暗暗下决心，一定要找机会到中国留学。

（4）A：＿＿＿＿＿＿＿＿＿＿＿＿＿＿＿＿＿＿？（怎样　才能）

B：凡是大学一、二年级的学生都可以报名参加政府奖学金考试，前十名的学生就有机会公费到中国留学。

（5）A：＿＿＿＿＿＿＿＿＿＿＿＿＿＿＿＿＿＿？（吗）

B：看到这个消息，我当然很高兴，于是第二天就去报了名。

（6）A：＿＿＿＿＿＿＿＿＿＿＿＿＿＿＿＿＿＿？

（考试　结果　怎样）

B：我考了个第三名。全家人都为我感到高兴，妈妈还流下了激动的眼泪。那时候我感觉我是世界上最幸福的人，我就要圆我的留学梦了。

（7）A：＿＿＿＿＿＿＿＿＿＿＿＿＿＿＿＿＿＿？

（现在　感觉　怎么样）

B：我感觉一切都是那么美好，一切都让我感到新鲜有趣。我在这里认识了很多朋友，我们常常一起玩儿、一起学习。我对汉语学习的热情越来越高，对中国的历史文化和风俗习惯也越来越感兴趣。

（8）A：________________________________？

（将来　什么　打算）

B：将来我可能当翻译，也可能当一个汉语教师。无论干什么，我都会成为连接我们国家和中国之间友谊的桥梁。

4. 复述这篇课文 Retell this text

（九）朗读中国经典诗词，请注意语音语调 Read aloud the classic Chinese poem and pay attention to the pronunciation and intonation

Huìchóng Chūn Jiāng Wǎnjǐng
惠崇　春　江　晚景

[Sòng] Sū Shì
[宋] 苏 轼（1037—1101）

Zhú wài táohuā sān-liǎng zhī, chūn jiāng shuǐ nuǎn yā xiān zhī.
竹 外 桃花 三两 枝，春 江 水 暖 鸭 先 知。

Lóuhāo mǎn dì lúyá duǎn, zhèng shì hétún yù shàng shí.
蒌蒿 满 地 芦芽 短， 正 是 河豚 欲 上 时。

（十）请欣赏下列著名的词句 Please enjoy the following famous saying

Zhī zhī wéi zhī zhī, bù zhī wéi bù zhī, shì zhì yě.
知之为知之，不知为不知，是知也。

Be certain of what you know and don't pretend to know things you don't, which is true wisdom.

Dì-wǔshíqī kè　Nǐ de àihào shì shénme

第五十七课　你的爱好是什么

Lesson 57　What's your hobby?

一　课文 Text

（口语课上，老师叫同学们谈谈自己的爱好）

老师：我先问问大家，你们都有什么爱好？谁先说？

戴维：老师，让我先说吧。

老师：好，你说吧。你的爱好是什么？

戴维：我喜欢摄影，将来想当记者。所以除了学习汉语，我还到一个摄影学校去学摄影。

老师：海伦呢？

海伦：我喜欢音乐。因为我爸爸是乐团指挥，妈妈是歌唱家，所以我从小就喜欢音乐。高中毕业时，我想考音乐学院，但没考上，却考上了外语学院，竟然还拿到了奖学金，来中国留学。现在，业余时间，我还是喜欢搞音乐。大学时我组织过一个乐队，我既是作曲，又是乐队指挥。我们乐队还公开演出过几次，连电视台都报道过。在我的家乡，我们乐队小有名气。来中国后，我对中国音乐产生了兴趣，业余时间，我跟一位老师学习中国民歌。

老师：真不简单。下面该谁说了？

美尼：老师，我来说说吧。我热爱文学，喜欢写作，从小就梦想当作家。所以，我几乎每天都写点儿东西。

老师：主要写什么？散文、诗歌还是小说？

美尼：主要写小说，有时候也写点儿散文和诗。

老师：发表过作品吗？

美尼：在我们国内的一家网站上发表过一些，但还没有出过书。

老师：有志者事竟成，只要坚持写下去，总有一天会成功的。等出书了，一定要给老师看看。

美尼：谢谢老师的鼓励。我来中国学习汉语，一方面是想读中国的文学作品，另一方面是想把中国作家的优秀作品翻译成我们国家的语言，让我们国家的读者也能读到好的中文作品。

老师：老师听了真高兴。阿宝呢？（阿宝正在打盹儿）阿宝，你也说说吧。

阿宝：老师，我的爱好是吃饭和睡觉。

戴维：吃饭和睡觉怎么能算爱好呢？这是每个人每天都要做的事儿呀。

阿宝：除了吃饭和睡觉，我还喜欢上网玩儿游戏。

老师：这也算是一种爱好吧。不过，不要玩儿疯了。昨天晚上是不是又玩儿到天亮才睡觉的？

阿宝：没有，就玩儿到三点。

大家：哈哈哈哈……

老师：难怪，困的话，趴桌子上再睡一会儿吧。不过，别打呼噜。

戴维：哈哈！老师的爱好是幽默。

二 生词 New Words

1	爱好	àihào	动、名	be fond of; hobby
2	摄影	shèyǐng	动	photograph; take a picture
3	歌唱家	gēchàngjiā	名	singer
	歌唱	gēchàng	动	sing
4	却	què	副	but; yet; however
5	乐队	yuèduì	名	band; orchestra
6	公开	gōngkāi	形、动	public; make public

7	演出	yǎnchū	动	perform; show
8	报道	bàodào	动、名	report
9	家乡	jiāxiāng	名	hometown
10	名气	míngqi	名	reputation; fame
11	民歌	míngē	名	folk song
12	热爱	rè'ài	动	love
13	文学	wénxué	名	literature
14	写作	xiězuò	动	write
15	作家	zuòjiā	名	writer; author
16	散文	sǎnwén	名	prose
17	诗歌	shīgē	名	poetry; poem
18	小说	xiǎoshuō	名	fiction; novel
19	网站	wǎngzhàn	名	website
20	发表	fābiǎo	动	publish (articles, paintings, songs, etc. in a periodical)
21	出书	chū shū		have (a book) published
22	有志者事竟成	yǒuzhìzhě shì jìng chéng		Where there's a will, there's a way.
23	一方面	yì fāngmiàn		on the one hand
24	另	lìng	代、副	another; in addition
25	优秀	yōuxiù	形	excellent; outstanding
26	打盹儿	dǎ dǔnr	动	doze off; take (or have) a nap
27	算	suàn	动	consider; regard as; count as
28	疯	fēng	动、形	play crazily; crazy
29	亮	liàng	形、动	shining

30 趴	pā	动	bend over; lean on
31 幽默	yōumò	形	humorous

三 注释 Notes

（一）却

“却”表示转折，语气较轻。例如：

“ 却 ” indicates a transition and is spoken in a light tone. For example:

1. 学到第四册，课文难是难了一点儿，却很有意思。
2. 对我来说，虽然每天都很忙，却感到生活很快乐。
3. 虽然是春天了，天气却还很冷。

（二）竟然

副词“竟然”表示没想到，出乎意料，还可以单说“竟”。在句中放在动词或形容词前面做状语。例如：

The adverb “竟然”, meaning “unexpectedly”, is also abbreviated as “竟”. It is usually put before a verb or an adjective as an adverbial in a sentence. For example:

1. 高中毕业时我想考音乐学院，竟然没考上。
2. 下这么大雨，我想他不会来了，没想到，他竟然来了。
3. 这次考试他竟然得了一百分。

（三）既……也 / 又

“既”常和“也、又”连用，表示不止一个方面，还有其他方面。例如：

“既” is often used together with “也” or “又” to indicate that something has more than one aspect. For example:

1. 我既是作曲，又是乐队指挥。
2. 他既会说英语，也会说法语。
3. 既要注意发音，也要注意声调。不然，你说的汉语中国人可能听不懂。

（四）有志者事竟成

“有志者事竟成”是个谚语，在句中单用，常用来激励自己和他人。

“有志者事竟成” is a proverb often used independently in a sentence to encourage oneself and others.

四 练习 Exercises

（一）朗读 Read aloud

1. 朗读下列发音相近的词语 Read aloud the following words with similar pronunciation

yuètuán 乐团	yuētán 约谈	zhǐhuī 指挥	zhìhuì 智慧
jìngrán 竟然	jǐngrán 井然	míngqi 名气	míngxì 明细
gǔlì 鼓励	gūlì 孤立	xiězuò 写作	xiézuò 协作

2. 朗读下列短语 Read the following phrases aloud

爱好：爱好文学　爱好音乐　爱好摄影　爱好书法
爱好足球　爱好游泳　爱好画画儿

既：既是作曲又是指挥　既是老师又是朋友
既会汉语也会英语　既是夫妻又是同事

热爱：热爱音乐　热爱文学　热爱生活　热爱艺术
热爱跳舞　热爱体育　热爱摄影

梦想：梦想当作家　梦想当演员　梦想当翻译
梦想当汉语教师　梦想当运动员

几乎：几乎没写　几乎摔倒　几乎没做完　几乎忘了　几乎没有

成功：祝你成功　争取成功　非常成功

难怪：难怪他没来　难怪他这样做　难怪你不知道
难怪她那么伤心

（二）替换并朗读 Replace and read aloud

1. 我喜欢摄影。

看书	写作	听音乐
跟朋友聊天儿		上网玩儿游戏
画画儿		旅游

2. 因为将来想当记者，所以，除了学习汉语之外，我还到一个摄影学校去学摄影。

喜欢中国功夫	我还在一个武术班练武术
热爱环保	我参加了环保志愿者组织
将来想当一个教师	我常去参观中国的学校
我喜欢旅游	我几乎走遍了大半个中国
我想当志愿者	周末常去养老院陪老爷爷老奶奶

3. 我想考音乐学院，却考上了外语学院。

我想游泳	来跑步了
我想去美国留学	来到了中国
我想学西医	学起了中医
他想当一个记者	成了汉语老师

4. 来中国以后，我又对中国音乐产生了兴趣。

太极拳	京剧	中国武术
中医	汉字书法	

（三）**选词填空并朗读下列句子** Choose the appropriate words to fill in the blanks and read aloud the following sentences

连　还　先　就　当　下去

1. 我先问问大家，你们都有什么爱好？谁________说？
2. 我喜欢摄影，将来想当记者。所以除了学习汉语，我________到一个摄影学校去学摄影。
3. 我喜欢音乐。因为我爸爸是乐团指挥，妈妈是歌唱家，所以我从小________喜欢音乐。高中毕业时，我想考音乐学院，竟然没考上，却考上了外语学院。
4. 业余时间，我还是喜欢搞音乐。大学时我组织过一个乐队，我既是作曲，又是乐队指挥。我们乐队还公开演出过好几次，________电视台都报道过。
5. 我热爱文学，喜欢写作，从小就梦想________作家。所以，几乎每天都写点儿东西。主要写小说，有时候也写点儿散文和诗。
6. 有志者事竟成，只要坚持写________，总有一天会成功的。等出书了，一定要给老师看看。

难怪　有志者事竟成　发表　成功　既　梦想

1. 她常在网上________自己写的小说。
2. 他利用暑假在一家旅游公司打工，________当翻译又当导游。
3. 他的________是当一个外交官。
4. 老师总是跟我们说，________，年轻人只要努力，只要坚持，就能梦想成真。
5. ________她那么喜欢音乐，原来她妈妈是歌唱家。
6. 很多人都希望自己能________，但并不是所有的人都明白，怎样才能________。

（四）完成下列句子并大声朗读 Complete the following sentences and read them aloud

1. 没想到，我写的字、画的画儿，________________。（竟然）

2. 期中考试，他________________。（竟然 得了）

3. 出国留学这么大的事儿，她________________。（竟然 连……也……）

4. 他既聪明又________________，所以成绩一直很好。

5. 希望同学们既要努力学习，________________。（也/又 身体）

6. 既要重视课堂学习，又要________________。（课外 中国人）

（五）完成下列会话并大声朗读 Complete the following conversations and read them aloud

1. A：戴维的爱好是什么？

   B：________________。（打球 摄影 音乐 书法 绘画）

2. A：海伦为什么那么喜欢音乐？

   B：________________。（因为）

3. A：来中国以后，海伦又对什么产生了兴趣？

   B：________________。（民歌）

4. A：美尼为什么每天都坚持写东西？

   B：________________。（梦想 作家）

5. A：老师是怎么鼓励美尼的？

   B：________________。

6. A：阿宝是个什么样的学生？

   B：________________。（上网）

7. A：你是老师的话，允许学生在课堂上睡觉吗？为什么？

   B：________________。

8. A：你觉得这个班怎么样？你愿意在这样的班里学习吗？

B：________________________________。

（六）将A、B两列连线，组成一个句子，然后朗读 Match A with B to make correct sentences and read aloud

1.

A	B
一方面要努力提高听说能力，	另一方面也要做个好女儿。
一方面我要学好汉语，	另一方面也要看到自己的不足。
一方面要看到自己的成绩，	另一方面也想跟他一起学好汉语。
一方面我想跟他交朋友，	另一方面也要好好锻炼身体。
一方面要努力学习，	另一方面我也要学好中医。
我一方面要当个好学生，	另一方面也要提高读写能力。

2.

A	B
你只要把汉语学好，	不管多贵我都买。
只要是遇见自己喜欢的书，	就一定感冒。
我只要一受凉，	就一定能实现当翻译的理想。
你只要跟他说说这件事，	我一定陪你好好玩儿几天。
你只要来，	回国后就能找到好工作。
你只要坚持下去，	他就一定会帮你想办法。

（七）和同学一起表演课文 Act out the text with your classmates

（八）自由表达 Express yourself freely

和同学一起，互相说说自己的业余爱好是什么。

（九）读后说 Read the passage and say it

1. 朗读 Read aloud

响遏行云

战国时秦国有个名叫薛谭的青年，很喜爱唱歌，声音也很好听。后来，他找到秦国著名的歌手秦青，拜他为师，立志要成为一名出色的歌唱家。经过一段时间的刻苦学习，他唱歌的水平有了很大的提高，自以为把老师的本领都学到手了。

一天，他对秦青说："老师，我学得差不多了，打算明天回去，您看行吗？"秦青本想进一步培养他，但看他自己觉得满足了，也就没有留他。

第二天，秦青在郊外准备了酒菜，为薛谭送行。在饮酒的时候，秦青打着拍子，唱了一支悲壮的歌曲。高亢的歌声、悠扬的旋律，响彻云霄，连天空中的云朵，都好像被歌声吸引而停止不动了。

薛谭听得十分入迷，也非常惊讶，他感到自己盲目自满是很愚蠢的。于是，他非常惭愧地说："老师，我原来以为跟您学得差不多了，现在才知道还差得很远。请老师原谅我，让我继续跟您学吧！"秦青听了，十分高兴，就又把他留下了。

经过多年的努力，薛谭终于也成了一名优秀的歌唱家。

小词典

响遏行云	xiǎng'è-xíngyún		(of singing) be so sonorous that it stops the passing clouds
拜师	bài shī	动	take sb. as a one's teacher
立志	lì zhì	动	be determined
出色	chūsè	形	excellent; extremely good
刻苦	kèkǔ	形	assiduous; hard-working
本领	běnlǐng	名	skill; ability
郊外	jiāowài	名	outskirt
送行	sòng xíng	动	see sb. off
拍子	pāizi	名	(of music) rhythm
悲壮	bēizhuàng	形	solemn and stirring
高亢	gāokàng	形	(of voice) loud and sonorous

悠扬	yōuyáng	形	melodious
旋律	xuánlǜ	名	melody
响彻云霄	xiǎngchè-yúnxiāo		(of sound) very loud and clear
吸引	xīyǐn	动	attract
入迷	rù mí	动	be fascinated; be absorbed
惊讶	jīngyà	形	surprised; astonished
盲目	mángmù	形	blind; aimless
自满	zìmǎn	形	feel complacent or self-satisfied
愚蠢	yúchǔn	形	stupid; foolish

专名

战国	Zhànguó	Warring States Period (475—221 BC)
秦国	Qín Guó	State of Qin (770—221 BC)
薛谭	Xuē Tán	name of a person
秦青	Qín Qīng	name of a person

2. 回答下列问题 Answer the following questions

（1）这个故事发生在什么时候？

（2）薛谭为什么要拜秦青为师？

（3）薛谭学得怎么样？

（4）薛谭为什么想回家？

（5）秦青怎么为薛谭送行？

（6）秦青的歌唱得怎么样？

（7）薛谭为什么感到惭愧？

（8）薛谭的愿望实现了没有？

（**提示**：不知道的词，请问百度 / 谷歌。）

3. 你是 A，请你向 B 提问 Supposing you are A, ask B questions

（1）A: ________________________________？（爱好）

B：薛谭很喜爱唱歌，而且声音也很好听。

（2）A: ________________________________？（拜　谁）

B：薛谭找到秦国著名的歌手秦青，拜他为师，立志要成为一名出色的歌唱家。

（3）A: ________________________________？（为什么）

B：因为薛谭以为把老师的本领都学到手了，所以就想回家。

（4）A: ________________________________？（……了吗）

B：秦青本来想进一步培养他，但看他自己觉得满足了，也就没有留他。

（5）A: ________________________________？（怎么　送行）

B：秦青在郊外准备了酒菜，为薛谭送行。在饮酒的时候，秦青打着拍子，唱了一支悲壮的歌曲。

（6）A: ________________________________？（怎么样）

B：秦青高亢的歌声、悠扬的旋律，响彻云霄，连天空中的云朵，都好像被歌声吸引而停止不动了。

（7）A: ________________________________？（为什么）

B：薛谭听了老师的歌，非常惊讶，他感到自己盲目自满是很愚蠢的。所以就请老师原谅他，让他继续跟老师学。

（8）A: ________________________________？（怎么样）

B：经过多年的努力，薛谭终于也成了一名优秀的歌唱家。

4. 复述这篇课文 Retell this text

（十）朗读中国经典诗词，请注意语音语调 Read aloud the classic Chinese poem and pay attention to the pronunciation and intonation

Guān Shū Yǒu Gǎn
观 书 有 感

[Sòng] Zhū Xī
[宋] 朱熹（1130—1200）

Bàn mǔ fāng táng yí jiàn kāi, tiānguāng yúnyǐng gòng páihuái.
半 亩 方 塘 一 鉴 开，天光 云影 共 徘徊。
Wèn qú nǎ dé qīng rú xǔ? Wèi yǒu yuántóu huó shuǐ lái.
问 渠 那 得 清 如 许？为 有 源头 活 水 来。

（十一）请欣赏下列著名的词句 Please enjoy the following famous saying

Shàng shàn ruò shuǐ. Shuǐ lì wànwù ér bù zhēng.
上 善 若 水。水 利 万 物 而 不 争。
The best virtue is like water's.
Water benefits everything, while never compete with them.

Dì-wǔshíbā kè 第五十八课 Lesson 58

Bǎohù rénlèi gòngtóng de jiāyuán——dìqiú 保护人类共同的家园——地球

Protect the common homeland of mankind—the earth

一 课文 Text

（吉米和马丁看了一个环保视频就聊了起来……）

马丁：看了这个视频，看到人类捕杀野生动物、砍伐森林、污染江河湖海，真让人痛心。

吉米：现在，环境问题是人类遇到的最大问题。要是再不重视环境保护，地球上可真要住不下去了。

马丁：气候在变暖、冰川在融化……，真让人为地球的命运担心。地球是人类共同的家园，如果地球的生态环境被破坏了，人类怎么生存？

吉米：可不是！要是抬头不见蓝天，河里没有鱼虾，地上没了森林和草原，也听不到小鸟的叫声，那么，人类可能也就完了。

马丁：真是太可怕了。

吉米：最可怕的是还有很多人没有意识到这种危险，还在不断地破坏环境，不断地制造生态灾难。

马丁：所以，要让更多的人知道保护环境的重要性，就必须从日常生活中的小事做起。

吉米：你不过是说得好听，可不让你开车你做得到吗？

马丁：做不到。

吉米：为了保护环境，我就不买车，坚持出门坐公共汽车。

马丁：坐公共汽车就不污染环境啦？公共汽车要是不用新能源，也污染环境。

吉米：比你开车总要好一些吧。

马丁：也好不了多少。

吉米：那你说怎么办啊？

马丁：我又不是科学家，哪儿知道怎么办？科学家们应该能想出好办法，比如开发新能源，用太阳能、风能什么的。

吉米：各国政府也应该尽力，保护好野生动物、保护好森林、保护好江河湖海。我想，人类一定会有办法的。

马丁：选举你当总统好了。

吉米：光当一个国家的总统有什么用？得当联合国秘书长，动员世界各国一起努力才行。

马丁：我想，新冠疫情可能会让人类觉醒过来，知道要尊重自然、保护自然、保护我们的地球家园。

吉米：新冠疫情可能会让全世界都明白，人类是祸福与共、命运相连的。只有各国团结起来，保护好我们的地球，人类才有美好的明天。

马丁：说得好！

二 生词 New Words

1	人类	rénlèi	名	mankind; human
2	共同	gòngtóng	形	common
3	家园	jiāyuán	名	home; homeland
4	地球	dìqiú	名	earth
5	捕杀	bǔshā	动	catch and kill (an animal)
6	野生	yěshēng	形	wild
7	砍伐	kǎnfá	动	log; lumber
8	森林	sēnlín	名	forest; woods

9	污染	wūrǎn	动	contaminate; pollute
10	痛心	tòngxīn	形	distressed; pained; grieved
11	重视	zhòngshì	动	attach importance to
12	冰川	bīngchuān	名	glacier
13	融化	rónghuà	动	melt
14	命运	mìngyùn	名	destiny
15	生态	shēngtài	名	ecology
16	破坏	pòhuài	动	destroy
17	生存	shēngcún	动	exist; live
18	蓝天	lán tiān		blue sky
19	草原	cǎoyuán	名	grassland
20	可怕	kěpà	形	horrible; dreadful; terrible
21	意识	yìshí	动、名	realize; be aware of; consciousness
22	制造	zhìzào	动	make
23	灾难	zāinàn	名	disaster; calamity
24	开发	kāifā	动	develop; exploit
25	能源	néngyuán	名	energy
26	太阳能	tàiyángnéng	名	solar energy
27	风能	fēngnéng	名	wind energy
28	选举	xuǎnjǔ	动	elect
29	总统	zǒngtǒng	名	president
30	秘书长	mìshūzhǎng	名	secretary-general
31	动员	dòngyuán	动	mobilize
32	觉醒	juéxǐng	动	awaken; realize
33	自然	zìrán	名、形、副	nature; natural; naturally

34 祸福与共	huòfú-yǔgòng		go through thick and thin together
35 相连	xiānglián	动	be tied (to); be bound up (with)
36 团结	tuánjié	动	unite

专名 Zhuānmíng Proper Nouns

1 联合国	Liánhéguó	United Nations
2 新冠疫情	Xīnguān Yìqíng	COVID-19 pandemic

三 注释 Notes

（一）动词 + 下去

趋向动词“下去”用在动词后面，表示动作由现在继续到将来。“动词+不+下去”则表示动作不能继续进行，是可能补语的否定形式。例如：

The directional verb “下去” is used after a verb to indicate that an action continues from the present to the future. “Verb + 不 + 下去”, which is the negative form of a potential complement, indicates that the action cannot continue. For example:

1. 明年我还想在这个学校学下去。
2. 要是再不保护环境，地球上可真要住不下去了。
3. 她说着说着就难过得说不下去了。

（二）不过

副词“不过”是“仅仅、只是”的意思，用来指明范围，含有往小里或往轻里说的意味，在句中做状语。例如：

The adverb “不过” means “just, only”. It is used to indicate the scope or range, implying it is not a big deal or insignificant. “不过” is used as an adverbial in a sentence. For example:

1. 你不过是说得好听，可不让你开车你做得到吗？
2. 她来中国留学的那年才不过十八岁。
3. 他不过是跟你开个玩笑，你不必当真。

（三）只有……才……

“只有”表示必需的、唯一的条件，没有这个条件，下面所说的目的就不能达到。常与“才”配合使用，组成一个条件复句。例如：

“只有” refers to the necessary and only condition, without which the purpose mentioned below cannot be achieved. It is often used with “才” to form a conditional complex sentence. For example:

1. 只有大家团结起来，保护好我们的地球，人类才有美好的明天。
2. 只有刻苦努力，不断练习，才能学好汉语。
3. 只有拿到 HSK 高级证书，才能进这家公司。

四 练习 Exercises

（一）朗读 Read aloud

1. 朗读下列发音相近的词语 Read aloud the following words with similar pronunciation

dìqiú 地球	qìqiú 气球	tòngxīn 痛心	dòng xīn 动 心
gòngtóng 共 同	gòngtōng 共 通	kǎnfá 砍伐	kànfǎ 看法
wūrǎn 污染	wù diǎn 误 点	kāifā 开发	kāi huā 开 花

2. 朗读下列短语 Read the following phrases aloud

共同：共同的家园　共同的心愿　共同的理想　共同的事业
　　　共同的爱好　共同的追求
生态：生态环境　生态科学　生态灾难　生态保护　保护地球生态
爱护：爱护自然　爱护野生动物　爱护环境　爱护公物　爱护地球
保护：保护环境　保护自然　保护儿童　保护地球——人类的家园
尊重：尊重老人　尊重历史　尊重事实　尊重科学　受人尊重
　　　非常尊重

开发：开发能力　开发新能源　开发新材料　新技术开发区
与共：祸福与共　生死与共　患难与共　荣辱与共

（二）**替换并朗读** Replace and read aloud

1. 看到人类捕杀野生动物、砍伐森林、污染江河湖海，真让人痛心。

全世界那么多人死于新冠疫情
全世界那么多人吃不饱饭
他病成这样
这条河里都是污水
这里环境被破坏成这样

2. 现在，环境问题是人类遇到的最大的问题。

汉语声调不准是不少留学生
读和写跟不上，是很多同学
成绩上不去可能得不到奖学金，是她
租不到房子是她
公司不同意让我再学一年，是我

3. 要是再这样，地球上可真要住不下去了。

你的身体会受不了的
他就得休学了
我就得回国了
他很难坚持再学一年

4. 要让更多的人知道保护环境的重要，就必须从日常生活中的小事做起。

从孩子们抓起
搞好环保宣传和环保教育
加强管理
严惩那些污染环境的个人和单位

5. 只有大家团结起来，保护好我们的地球，人类才有美好的明天。

全世界各国和平共处
维护世界永久和平
努力发展经济，消灭贫困
世界各国相互尊重，合作共赢

（三）**选词填空并朗读下列句子** Choose the appropriate words to fill in the blanks and read aloud the following sentences

融化　捕杀　砍伐　相连　污染　可怕

1. 中国的《野生动物保护法》明确禁止________野生动物。
2. 要是随便________森林，一定会造成生态灾难。
3. 冰川开始________，这是地球变暖造成的。
4. 这里的河流都已被________，河里已经没有了鱼虾。
5. 最________的是，很多人没有环保意识，更没有环保习惯。
6. 新冠疫情让全世界人民认识到，人类的命运是________的。

（四）**完成下列句子并大声朗读** Complete the following sentences and read them aloud

1. 如果这里的环境再继续恶化，________________。（动词＋不＋下去）
2. 只要________________，就一定能实现你的理想。（动词＋下去）
3. 我________________，并不打算买。（不过）
4. 他________________，你不必在意。（不过）
5. 只有不怕困难、坚持上课、刻苦练习，________________。（才）
6. ________________，才能升入二年级，继续学习。（只有）

（五）**完成下列会话并大声朗读** Complete the following conversations and read them aloud

1. A：你觉得人类都面临着哪些环境问题？
   B：____________________________________。

2. A：课文说："最可怕的是还有很多人没有意识到地球正面临着环境危险，还在不断地制造生态灾难。"你同意这一说法吗？请举例说明。

B：____。

3. A：为了保护环境，我们怎样从自己日常生活的小事做起？

B：____。

4. A：什么时候用"你不过是说得好听"这个句子？

B：____。

5. A：你觉得新冠疫情问题能不能让人类觉醒过来？

B：____。

6. A：吉米希望世界各国都明白什么？你同意他的意见吗？

B：____。

（六）和同学一起表演课文 Act out the text with your classmates

（七）自由表达 Express yourself freely

和同学一起谈谈环境问题，说说你对保护环境的看法。

（八）读后说 Read the passage and say it

1. 朗读 Read aloud

狼也有情

这是一个地质工程师亲身经历的故事。

一次，他们地质队开车回昆明送材料，为了安全，车上还有战士带枪保护他们。糟糕的是，那天遇上下大雪，经过一座山时，车轮突然陷进一个雪坑里，直打滑，怎么也开不出来。

正在他们十分着急的时候，不知道从什么地方跑出来一群狼。战士想开枪打死这些狼，但是被经验丰富的队长制止了。队长告诉大家，无论如何都不能开枪。如果开枪打死一只狼，就会从森林里跑出来一群狼，那么今天谁都跑不了。他说，狼是饿了，想吃东西，快把车上带的肉扔下去，给它们吃。

正好车上带了不少肉，是地质队员们往昆明家里带的，于是大家把肉扔了下去。狼看见肉，就跑过来吃了起来。可它们吃饱了后，还没有要走的意思，大家不知道该怎么办了。

正在他们感到绝望的时候，只见头狼带着那群狼跑进了森林。他们马上把车发动起来，想快点儿离开，但是车轮还是打滑出不来。

这时，那群狼又回来了。只见每只狼嘴里都叼着一根枯树枝，在头狼的带领下，它们把树枝垫在车轮下。然后，这群狼有的用嘴拱，有的用尾巴扫，把车前的雪都扫干净了。看到这种情况，大家都惊呆了。之后，大家就一起下车，把车推出了雪坑，顺利回到了昆明。

这个真实的故事，听起来既有点儿惊险，又生动地说明了狼这样的动物也是有感情的。我们总以为狼是凶恶的，然而这些狼是多么有情有义啊！可见，我们人类对野生动物实在是太不了解了。

小词典

狼	láng	名	wolf
地质	dìzhì	名	geology
战士	zhànshì	名	soldier
枪	qiāng	名	gun
车轮	chēlún	名	wheel
陷	xiàn	动	sink into
坑	kēng	名、动	hole; pit defraud
直	zhí	副、形	continuously; straight
打滑	dǎhuá	动	slip
群	qún	量	pack; throng
制止	zhìzhǐ	动	stop
绝望	jué wàng	动	despair
头狼	tóuláng	名	alpha wolf; leader wolf

发动	fādòng	动	start up
叼	diāo	动	hold in the mouth
树枝	shùzhī	名	twig; branch
带领	dàilǐng	动	lead; guide
垫	diàn	动	pad
拱	gǒng	动	(of an animal) dig with the snout
尾巴	wěiba	名	tail
惊呆	jīngdāi		stupefied; stunned
惊险	jīngxiǎn	形	breathtaking; thrilling
生动	shēngdòng	形	vivid; lively
凶恶	xiōng'è	形	fierce; ferocious
有情有义	yǒuqíng-yǒuyì		having affection and faith
可见	kějiàn	连	it shows; that proves

2. 回答下列问题 Answer the following questions

（1）这是谁经历的故事？

（2）他们那天要回昆明做什么？

（3）汽车在路上遇到了什么麻烦？

（4）狼为什么突然从森林里跑了出来？

（5）队长为什么不让战士开枪打狼？

（6）队长让大家怎么对待这群狼？

（7）狼吃饱了以后，又去哪儿了？

（8）头狼带着狼群去树林里干了什么？

（9）这群狼是怎么帮助他们的？

（10）这个故事说明了什么？

3. 你是 A，请你向 B 提问 Supposing you are A, ask B questions

（1）A：________________________________？

B：那天我们地质队开车回昆明送材料。

（2）A：____？

B：为了安全，车上还有战士带枪保护我们。

（3）A：____？

B：糟糕的是，那天赶上下大雪，在经过一座山时，车轮突然陷进一个雪坑里，直打滑，怎么也开不出来了。

（4）A：____？

B：正在我们十分着急的时候，不知道从什么地方跑出来一群狼。

（5）A：____？

B：战士想开枪打死这些狼，但是被队长制止了。队长告诉大家，无论如何都不能开枪。如果开枪打死一只狼，就会从森林里跑出来一群狼。那么今天我们谁都跑不了。

（6）A：____？

B：队长说，狼是饿了，想吃东西，快把车上带的肉扔下去，给它们吃。

（7）A：____。

B：正好车上带了不少肉，是地质队员们往昆明家里带的，于是大家把肉扔了下去。狼看见肉，就一起吃了起来。

（8）A：____？

B：可狼吃饱了后，还没有要走的意思，我们不知道该怎么办了。

（9）A：____？

B：正在我们感到绝望的时候，只见头狼带着那群狼跑进了森林。

（10）A：____？

B：看到狼进了森林，我们赶快把车发动起来，想快点儿离开，但是车轮还是打滑出不来。

（11）A：____？

B：这时，我们看到那群狼又回来了，每只狼嘴里都叼着一根干树枝。在头狼的带领下，它们把树枝垫在车轮下。然后，这群狼用嘴拱、用尾巴扫，把车前的雪扫干净了。

（12）A：______________________________？

B：看到这种情况，我们全都惊呆了，完全没想到狼竟然会这么干。

（13）A：______________________________？

B：之后，大家一起从车上下来，把车推出了雪坑，顺利回到了昆明。

（14）A：______________________________？

B：这个真实的故事生动地说明，连狼这样的动物也是有感情的。我们总以为狼是凶恶的，然而，这群狼却那么有情有义。可见，我们人类对野生动物实在是太不了解了。

4. 复述这篇课文 Retell this text

（九）朗读中国经典诗词，请注意语音语调 Read aloud the classic Chinese poem and pay attention to the pronunciation and intonation

Niǎo
鸟

[Táng] Bái Jūyì
［唐］白居易（772—846）

Shuí dào qún shēng xìngmìng wēi,　yìbān gǔ ròu yìbān pí.
谁道群生性命微，一般骨肉一般皮。

Quàn jūn mò dǎ zhī tóu niǎo,　zǐ zài cháo zhōng wàng mǔ guī.
劝君莫打枝头鸟，子在巢中望母归。

（十）请欣赏下列著名的词句 Please enjoy the following famous saying

Huò xī fú zhī suǒ yǐ,　fú xī huò zhī suǒ fú.
祸兮福之所倚，福兮祸之所伏。

Luck and misfortune come in turn.

Dì-wǔshíjiǔ kè 第五十九课 Lesson 59

Kuài jiào bǎ tā sòngdào yīyuàn qu 快叫120，把她送到医院去 Call 120 and take her to the hospital quickly

一 课文 Text

（一）快叫120，赶快把她送到医院去

（玛丽突然病了，山本和吴丹陪她去医院……）

山本：吴丹，快！快！你快来呀。

吴丹：山本，怎么了？

山本：不知道怎么回事儿，玛丽突然肚子疼了，而且疼得很厉害。我给她量了一下体温，已经39度5了。

吴丹：你别着急，我马上就过去。

（吴丹到了）

山本：你看，怎么办呢？

吴丹：快叫120，赶快把她送到医院去。

（山本给120打电话）

山本：喂，120吗？这里是语言大学留学生第三公寓楼，二门，806号。我们这里有个同学病了，请你们赶快派车来。

120：知道了，我们大约十分钟到。

山本：玛丽，你坚持一下，急救车马上就到。

（120急救车到了）

大夫：你哪儿不舒服？

玛丽：（指自己的肚子）这儿。

大夫：啊，可能是急性阑尾炎。

（对护士）快！把她抬到车上去。（对山本和吴丹）你们两个也跟着一起去吧，说不定要做手术。

（二）多亏你们来得及时

（检查以后）

大夫：是急性阑尾炎，什么时候感觉不舒服的？

玛丽：今天上午，我以为是胃里不舒服，没有想到是阑尾炎。

大夫：阑尾炎开始的时候，常常让病人觉得是胃不舒服。你现在发烧到40度，是急性发作，要马上住院，做切除手术。

山本：啊，这么严重。

大夫：多亏你们来得及时，不然就危险了。不过，这是个小手术，术后三四天就可以出院了。你们谁去办一下住院手续，还要有家属签字。

山本：这里没有家属，我们都是留学生。老师可以代替家属签字吗？我已经给老师打电话了，她马上就到。

大夫：可以。

（手术后）

山本：大夫，手术怎么样？

大夫：很好，很成功，三四天就可以出院了，请放心吧。

山本：是吗？那太好了！可把我吓坏了。

二　生词 New Words

1 陪	péi	动	keep company; accompany
2 量	liáng	动	measure
3 体温	tǐwēn	名	(body) temperature
4 赶快	gǎnkuài	副	at once; quickly
5 派	pài	动	send; dispatch

6	急救车	jíjiùchē	名	ambulance
	急救	jíjiù	动	(give) first-aid to sb.
7	急性	jíxìng	形	acute
8	阑尾炎	lánwěiyán	名	appendicitis
9	说不定	shuōbudìng	副	perhaps; maybe
10	手术	shǒushù	名	operation; surgery
11	以为	yǐwéi	动	think; believe; consider
12	胃	wèi	名	stomach
13	发烧	fā shāo	动	have a fever
14	发作	fāzuò	动	(of latent things) act up; suddenly break out or show effect
15	切除	qiēchú	动	remove; cut off
16	严重	yánzhòng	形	serious; critical
17	及时	jíshí	形	timely
18	不然	bùrán	连、形	or else; if not; otherwise
19	危险	wēixiǎn	形	dangerous
20	出院	chū yuàn	动	be discharged from hospital
	住院	zhù yuàn	动	be hospitalized
21	家属	jiāshǔ	名	family member
22	签字	qiān zì	动	sign; write one's signature
23	代替	dàitì	动	take the place of

三 注释 Notes

（一）急救电话：120

“120”是中国的急救电话。如果突然发病，可以拨打这个电话，急救中心会马上派人和车，把病人送到医院。

“120” is the emergency number in China. If you get sick suddenly, you can dial this number. The emergency center will immediately send personnel and an ambulance to take the patient to the hospital.

（二）说不定

“说不定”是副词，表示估计。例如：

“说不定” is an adverb indicating estimation. For example:

1. 你们两个也一起去吧，说不定需要做手术。
2. 他现在不来，说不定有什么事了。
3. 我们快走吧，说不定他们已经早到了，正在等我们呢。

（三）不然

“不然”是连词，表示假设，意思是：如果不这样。后边接表示结果的小句，有时可以带“的话”，加强假设的语气。例如：

The conjunction “不然” indicates assumption, meaning “otherwise”. It is followed by a clause indicating the result, and sometimes it can be followed by “的话” to reinforce the hypothetical tone. For example:

1. 多亏你们来得及时，不然就危险了。
2. 我得通过这个考试，不然的话得不到奖学金。
3. 我们得坐飞机去，不然来不及。

“不然”还是个形容词，用作谓语，前面可以有副词。也可以用在句子的开头，表示否定对方的说法。例如：

“不然” is also an adjective. It is used as a predicate and can be preceded by an adverb. It can also be used at the beginning of a sentence to negate the other person’s statement. For example:

1. 你看他像是中国人，其实<u>不然</u>，他是韩国人。

2. A：你们家乡是不是也这么冷？

   B：<u>不然</u>，我们家乡没有冬天，四季如春。

（四）坏

形容词“坏”在句中做动词的结果补语，表示程度深。“吓坏了”的意思是非常担心和害怕。类似的说法有“饿坏了（非常饿）、冻坏了（很冷）、气坏了（非常生气）、忙坏了（非常忙）、乐坏了（非常高兴）”等。例如：

The adjective “坏” is used as a result complement of the verb in a sentence, indicating a high level. “吓坏了” refers to being very worried and afraid. Similar expressions include “饿坏了” (very hungry), “冻坏了” (very cold), “气坏了” (very angry), “忙坏了” (very busy) and “乐坏了” (very happy), etc. For example:

1. 这次可真把我吓<u>坏</u>了。
2. 听到弟弟考上了大学，爸爸妈妈可乐<u>坏</u>了。
3. 他可把我气<u>坏</u>了。
4. 昨天出去没穿羽绒服，可把我冻<u>坏</u>了。
5. 早上没吃东西，可把我饿<u>坏</u>了。
6. 他这么一说，把我们乐<u>坏</u>了。

四 练习 Exercises

（一）朗读 Read aloud

1. 朗读下列发音相近的词语 Read aloud the following words with similar pronunciation

tǐwēn 体温	tíwèn 提问	jíxìng 急性	jìxing 记性
shǒushù 手术	shǒushū 手书	yǐwéi 以为	yìwèi 意味
jíshí 及时	jíshǐ 即使	fàng xīn 放心	fánxīn 烦心

2. 朗读下列短语 Read the following phrases aloud

量：量体温　量体重　量身高　量血压　量血糖

急性：急性阑尾炎　急性肠炎　急性肝炎　急性发作

抬：抬上来　抬起来　抬进来　抬进去　抬不动　抬得动

严重：很严重　病得很严重　伤得很严重　情况很严重　事故很严重

多亏：多亏你没去　多亏你在　多亏警察来了　多亏这位好心人

及时：很及时　及时赶到　到得很及时　手术很及时

顺利：祝你顺利　工作顺利　非常顺利　一切顺利　都很顺利

放心：不放心　很放心　你放心吧　放不下心

（二）**替换并朗读** Replace and read aloud

1. 快叫120，赶快把她送到医院去。

出租车　老师　两个同学

2. 快，把她抬到车上去。

这些书搬到楼上去
这个行李箱送到房间去
爸爸送到医院去

3. 你们两个也一起去吧，说不定需要做手术。

能帮上她的忙
她希望你们去呢
病人需要你们照顾

4. 多亏你们来得及时，不然就危险了。

大夫及时给她做了手术	就危险了
有手机导航	我们真不知道怎么走了
你叫醒我	又迟到了
我们坐上了这辆车	就赶不上了

5. 可把我吓坏了。

饿	乐	气	累
忙	渴	冻	

（三）**选词填空并朗读下列句子** Choose the appropriate words to fill in the blanks and read aloud the following sentences

抬　给　及时　成功　体温　把

1. 不知道怎么回事儿，玛丽突然肚子疼了，而且疼得很厉害。我给她量了一下________，已经烧到 39 度 5 了。
2. 快叫 120，赶快________她送到医院去。
3. 快！把她________到车上去。你们两个也跟着一起去吧，说不定要住院做手术。
4. 多亏你们来得________，不然就危险了。不过，这是个小手术，术后三四天就可以出院了。
5. 我们都是留学生，老师可以代替家属签字吗？我已经________老师打电话了，她马上就到。
6. 手术很________，三四天就可以出院了，请放心吧。

急性　量　以为　及时　把　说不定

1. 我________了________体重，这个月减了两公斤。
2. 昨天他得了________肠炎，一个晚上拉了好几次。
3. 看这天，________要下雨，还是带上伞吧。
4. 你________学习一门外语那么容易呢，不下苦功夫是学不好的。
5. 昨天晚上他喝多了，是我们几个人________他抬上出租车拉回来的。
6. 急性阑尾炎只要发现得早，________做手术，是可以治好的。

（四）完成下列句子并大声朗读 Complete the following sentences and read them aloud

1. 要考试了，我得好好复习，＿＿＿＿＿＿＿＿＿＿＿＿。（不然）
2. 这个假期我一定得去南方旅行一次，＿＿＿＿＿＿＿＿＿＿＿＿。（不然）
3. 我要向她说一声"对不起"，＿＿＿＿＿＿＿＿＿＿＿＿。（不然）
4. 你打个电话问问他，＿＿＿＿＿＿＿＿＿＿＿＿。（说不定）
5. 今天你千万别把手机调成静音，＿＿＿＿＿＿＿＿＿＿＿＿。（说不定）
6. 这件事儿虽然我没有告诉他，但＿＿＿＿＿＿＿＿＿＿＿＿。（说不定）

（五）完成下列会话并大声朗读 Complete the following conversations and read them aloud

1. A：玛丽怎么了？
   B：＿＿＿＿＿＿＿＿＿＿＿＿。（突然）
2. A：吴丹来以后是怎么做的？
   B：＿＿＿＿＿＿＿＿＿＿＿＿。（给……打电话 / 叫 120）
3. A：120 的大夫认为玛丽是什么病？
   B：＿＿＿＿＿＿＿＿＿＿＿＿？（可能）
4. A：大夫为什么叫吴丹和山本也一起去医院？
   B：＿＿＿＿＿＿＿＿＿＿＿＿。（说不定）
5. A：大夫，她的病很严重吗？有没有危险？
   B：＿＿＿＿＿＿＿＿＿＿＿＿。（多亏　不然）
6. A：＿＿＿＿＿＿＿＿＿＿＿＿？（怎么样）
   B：手术做得很好，很成功，三四天就可以出院了。

（六）和同学一起表演课文 Act out the text with your classmates

（七）自由表达 Express yourself freely

和同学一起说说自己得病的经历。

（八）**读后说** Read the passage and say it

1. 朗读 Read aloud

玛丽住院了

昨天晚上玛丽突然病了，我给她量了量体温，一看39度5，烧得很厉害，可把我吓坏了。我不知道该怎么办才好，于是给吴丹打了电话。吴丹接到电话后就来了。她一看玛丽病成这个样子，连忙给120急救中心打电话，请他们赶快派救护车。不到10分钟，120的救护车就来了。我们帮护士把玛丽抬上了车，大夫对我们说："你们也一起去吧。看样子，她得的是急性阑尾炎，说不定要做手术。"我又赶快给林老师打电话，林老师让我们先去，她随后就到。

到了医院，经过大夫的诊断，果然是急性阑尾炎。大夫说要马上手术。这时林老师也赶来了，老师问大夫有没有什么危险，要不要通知家属。大夫说，多亏我们来得及时，不然就危险了，不过现在没有问题了，切除阑尾是小手术，术后三四天就可以出院。

林老师代替家属签了字，我们跑上跑下地给玛丽办完了住院手续，护士就把玛丽推进了手术室。林老师让我们回去休息，她一个人在医院等手术做完再回去。我和吴丹说，要和老师一起等。

一个多小时后，手术做完了，护士把玛丽推进了病房。大夫告诉我们，手术做得很顺利，三四天以后就可以出院，让我们放心。

林老师听了高兴地说："谢谢大夫。"大夫也对林老师说："你也不容易呀，我看你急得像自己的女儿得了病一样。"林老师忙说："是！是！"

小词典

连忙	liánmáng	副	at once
经过	jīngguò	动、名	after; through
诊断	zhěnduàn	动	diagnose
赶	gǎn	动	hurry

通知	tōngzhī	动、名	inform; notice
推	tuī	动	push
病房	bìngfáng	名	ward (of a hospital)

2. 回答下列问题 Answer the follwing questions

（1）玛丽发烧到多少度？

（2）山本为什么连忙给吴丹打电话？

（3）大夫说玛丽得的是什么病？

（4）大夫给玛丽做的是什么手术？

（5）山本和吴丹忙着做什么？

（6）手术做了多长时间？

（7）谁在手术室外边等着玛丽做完手术？

问问百度 / 谷歌：阑尾炎的症状是什么？阑尾炎手术是不是小手术？（要求用中文或汉语拼音写出你想说的话，读给老师和同学听。）

3. 你是 A，请你向 B 提问 Supposing you are A, ask B questions

（1）A：______________________________？

（你　怎么知道）

B：山本给我打来电话，我才知道玛丽病了。

（2）A：______________________________？（多少）

B：玛丽发烧快到 40 度了。

（3）A：______________________________？（怎么了）

B：玛丽发烧到 40 度，把山本吓坏了。

（4）A：______________________________？（有没有）

B：这是一个小手术，没有什么危险。

（5）A：______________________________？

（为什么　感谢）

B：林老师听大夫说手术很成功，高兴地向大夫表示感谢。

（6）A：________________________________?

（什么时候　能）

B：三四天后就可以出院了。

（7）A：________________________________?（怎么样）

B：林老师很着急，就像自己的女儿病了一样。

4. 复述这篇课文 Retell this text

（九）朗读中国经典诗词，请注意语音语调 Read aloud the classic Chinese poem and pay attention to the pronunciation and intonation

Zhúzhī Cí

竹枝 词

[Táng] Liú Yǔxī

[唐] 刘 禹锡（772—842）

Yángliǔ qīngqīng jiāngshuǐ píng，wén láng jiāng shàng chànggēshēng.

杨柳　青青　江水　平，闻　郎　江　上　唱歌声。

Dōngbiān rì chū xībiān yǔ，　dào shì wú qíng què yǒu qíng.

东边　日出西边雨，道　是　无　晴　却　有　晴。

（十）请欣赏下列著名的词句 Please enjoy the following famous saying

Qián shì bú wàng，hòu shì zhī shī.

前　事　不　忘，后　事　之师。

Past experience, if not forgotten, is a guide for the future.

Dì-liùshí kè 第六十课 Lesson 60

Kàn yàngzi nǐ qìsè búcuò 看样子你气色不错 You look good

一 课文 Text

（山本和罗兰要去医院看玛丽）

山本：下午我们去医院看看玛丽吧。

罗兰：好啊。

山本：给她带点儿什么去好呢？

罗兰：带一束鲜花吧。

（在医院病房）

山本：怎么样？你觉得。

玛丽：好多了。

山本：看样子你气色不错。刀口还疼吗？

玛丽：不疼了，就是有点儿痒。

山本：那就是快好了。这儿的条件怎么样？

玛丽：非常好，大夫和护士特别和蔼亲切，待病人就像亲人一样。

罗兰：要不要给你做点儿什么吃的送来？

玛丽：不用，太麻烦了。

罗兰：麻烦什么，你想吃什么就说吧，我给你做。

玛丽：真的不用，再说我现在没一点儿胃口。这两天一直打点滴，今天大夫才让我喝了点儿稀粥，等过两天出去以后再说吧。

山本：什么时候能出院，大夫说了吗？

玛丽：估计下个星期差不多了，要不是有点儿感染，早出去了。

山本：听大夫的，好好养着，别急着出院。

玛丽：落了好几天课了，怎么能不着急呢？回去可以一边上课，一边养嘛。

山本：那倒也是。好了，我们该走了，过两天再来看你。

玛丽：不用了，过两天说不定我就出院了，你们还想让我老在医院待着呀。

罗兰：那我们来接你。

玛丽：谢谢！

二 生词 New Words

1	气色	qìsè	名	complexion
2	束	shù	量	bundle; bunch
3	刀口	dāokǒu	名	cut; incision
4	痒	yǎng	形	itchy
5	条件	tiáojiàn	名	condition
6	和蔼	hé'ǎi	形	nice; kind
7	病人	bìngrén	名	patient
8	胃口	wèikǒu	名	appetite
9	打点滴	dǎ diǎndī		have an intravenous drip
10	稀	xī	形	watery; thin
11	粥	zhōu	名	porridge
12	估计	gūjì	动	estimate; appraise; reckon
13	感染	gǎnrǎn	动	infect
14	养	yǎng	动	recover; recuperate

15 老	lǎo	副	always; all the time
16 待	dāi	动	stay

三 注释 Notes

（一）怎么样

疑问代词"怎么样"用于询问情况、状态和性质。例如：

The interrogative pronoun "怎么样" is used to ask about a situation, state, or nature. For example:

1. 这种手机怎么样？
2. 你爸爸身体怎么样？
3. 你觉得他太极拳打得怎么样？

"怎么样 + 了"用于询问变化了的情况及其结果。例如：

"怎么样 + 了" is used to ask about a changed situation and its consequence. For example:

1. 你去留学的手续办得怎么样了？
2. 听说她住院了，现在怎么样了？
3. 来了一年多了，你现在汉语说得怎么样了？
4. A：你爸爸最近身体怎么样了？（此前爸爸身体不太好）
   B：好多了。

（二）多

"多"用在形容词后做补语，表示相差的程度大，有比较的意思。"好多了"的意思是：比过去好了很多。例如：

"多" is used after an adjective as a complement to indicate a big difference, implying a comparison. "好多了" means something is much better than it used to be. For example:

1. 你爸爸的身体现在好多了。
2. 她才二十岁，我都四十了，比她大多了。
3. 跟其他车比，这种车贵多了。

4. 别从那儿走了，从这儿走近多了。

5. 你最近瘦多了。

（三）不……了

“不……了”表示情况或意愿的变化。例如：

“不……了” indicates a change in situation or intention. For example:

1. 刀口已经不痒了。（以前痒）
2. 他不在这个学校了。（以前在这个学校）
3. 她刚才来电话说，今天不来了。（原来说今天要来）
4. 今天已经不发烧了。（昨天还发烧）

（四）再说

连词“再说”表示进一步说明原因或理由。例如：

The conjunction “再说” indicates a further explanation of the cause or reason. For example:

1. 我的刀口还没全好，再说我也不想吃东西。
2. 天已经很晚了，再说还下着雨，你就别走了。

（五）倒

副词“倒”是个多义词，课文里的“倒”用在肯定句中，主要起舒缓语气的作用。例如：

The adverb “倒” is a polysemous word. In the text, it is used in an affirmative sentence to moderate the tone. For example:

1. A：落了好几天课了，怎么能不着急呢？回去可以一边上课，一边养嘛。
   B：那倒也是。
2. 这个菜放了点儿醋倒挺好吃的。
3. 你们姐妹俩一起来留学倒不错，可以互相照顾。
4. 你这种说法倒挺新鲜的。

四 练习 Exercises

（一）朗读 Read aloud

1. 朗读下列发音相近的词语 Read aloud the following words with similar pronunciation

xiānhuā 鲜花	xiàn huā 献 花	qìsè 气色	qǐsè 起色
dāokǒu 刀口	dàokǒu 道口	gūjì 估计	gǔjì 古迹

2. 朗读下列短语 Read the following phrases aloud

看样子：看样子气色不错　看样子要下雨　看样子他不来了　看样子很新鲜

不错：身体不错　条件不错　说得不错　学得不错　写得不错　画得不错

麻烦：很麻烦　太麻烦　不麻烦　麻烦什么　麻烦你了　给你添麻烦了

胃口：胃口很好　胃口不错　没有胃口　不合我的胃口

估计：估计快了　估计他该来了　估计要下雨　估计下个星期出院

（二）替换并朗读 Replace and read aloud

1. 带<u>一束鲜花</u>去吧。

> 一些水果和面包
> 一本小说
> 护照和学生证
> 一些钱或信用卡

2. A：怎么样了？
   B：<u>好</u>多了。

> 快　暖和　舒服
> 轻松　安静

3. 看样子气色不错。

精神	身体	心情
天气	环境	条件

4. 就是有点儿痒。

想家	不舒服	难
困	忙	累

5. 这儿的条件怎么样？

食堂的饭菜	那儿的气候
医院的环境	留学生公寓
你最近身体	你爸爸妈妈

6. 估计下个星期差不多能出院了。

能考80多分	吉米明天能来
他会同意去	老师最近没时间
明天会下雪	他有什么事

（三）**选词填空并朗读下列句子** Choose the appropriate words to fill in the blanks and read aloud the following sentences

有点儿　感染　一边　打　了　什么

1. A：下午我们去医院看看玛丽吧。给她带点儿________去好呢？
   B：带一束鲜花吧。
2. A：看样子你气色不错。刀口还疼吗？
   B：不疼了，就是________痒。
3. A：要不要给你做点儿什么吃的送来？
   B：我现在没胃口。这几天一直________点滴，今天大夫才让我喝了点儿稀粥，等过两天出去以后再说吧。
4. A：什么时候能出院，大夫说________吗？
   B：估计下个星期差不多了，要不是有点儿________，早出去了。

5. A：听大夫的，好好养着，别急着出院。
   B：落了好几天课了，怎么能不着急呢？回去可以________上课，一边养嘛。

束　麻烦　痒　打点滴　气色　胃口

1. 她给自己喜欢的歌手送上了一________鲜花。
2. 我看爸爸最近________很不错，精神很好。
3. 腿上被蚊子（wénzi, mosquito）叮（dīng, sting; bite）了一下，特别________。
4. 她不愿意________别人，所以病了也不说，就一个人在宿舍躺着。
5. 他的________特别好，什么都能吃，吃什么都不胖。
6. 住院前几天，连稀粥都不能喝，只能________。

（四）完成下列句子并大声朗读 Complete the following sentences and read them aloud

1. 这天看样子要下雨，你最好________________。
2. 她整天快快乐乐的，________________。（看样子）
3. 我们还是坐地铁去吧，地铁快，________________。（再说）
4. 学习汉语，发音和声调非常重要，________________，中国人也听不懂啊。（再说）
5. 太晚了，明天再给他打电话吧，________________。（再说　关机　睡觉）
6. 这件事不着急，________________。（再说）

（五）完成下列会话并大声朗读 Complete the following conversations and read them aloud

1. A：下午我们到医院去看看她吧。
   B：________________________。
2. A：给她带点儿什么东西去呢？
   B：________________________。

3. A：你现在感觉怎么样？
   B：____。
   （很好 / 好多了 / 还不太好 / 还有点儿发烧）
4. A：看样子气色不错，肚子还疼吗？
   B：____？（不……了）
5. A：这儿的条件怎么样？
   B：____。
   （很好 / 马马虎虎 / 还可以）
6. A：什么时候能出院，大夫说了吗？
   B：____。（估计）

（六）和同学一起表演课文 Act out the text with your classmates

（七）读后说 Read the passage and say it

1. 朗读 Read aloud

普通人家

我是去年秋天到中国大连来学习中文的。大连是个美丽的城市。可是，这里的一切对我来说都是陌生的，所以为了更好地了解中国，我努力地寻找跟中国人交流的机会。

一天，我路过一家饭店，正好肚子也饿了，就走了进去。这个饭店不大，但是收拾得很干净。老板是个大胖子，爱说爱笑，笑起来的样子像个弥勒佛，老板娘也是个和善的阿姨。他们知道我是外国人，就热情地给我介绍店里的饭菜。他们的饭菜很好吃。临走时，老板拿出一张名片，对我说："你们学校离这里很近，你想吃什么就来吧，我们给你做。来不了的话，就打个电话，可以给你送过去。你离开家，到我们中国来不容易，要保重身体。吃好了，身体就好；身体好了，你父母也就放心了。"听了他的话，我心里感到暖暖的。

后来我就经常去这家饭店吃饭。每次老板都会来到我身边，跟我聊一会儿。开始，我只能听他说，自己想说的话都说不出来。慢慢地我也能用汉语跟他们交流了，心里很高兴。就这样，我们成了朋友，还互相加了微信。

那天，我感冒了，头重脚轻的，不想吃东西。老板知道后，就做了一碗热汤面给我送过来，非要我吃下去不可。他说："不吃东西怎么行？"一连几天，他都给我送来可口的饭菜，直到我病好。这让我非常感动。

有一次，他说周末要开车带我出去玩儿，我答应了。可是出发的前一天，我的左手因为打球受伤了。但是我不想失约，还是跟他们去了。一路上他们夫妇把我照顾得很好，我玩儿得很开心。回来以后，他们常给我发微信问我的情况。我感觉，他们对我就像对待自己的亲人一样。

我把自己的经历告诉了我的朋友。开始他不太相信，后来，他跟我一起去这个饭店吃饭，亲身感受到了那对夫妇的亲切和热情。于是，朋友也喜欢上了这爱说爱笑的老板一家。

我马上就要回国了。我想，回国以后我也忘不了这个小饭馆，忘不了这对中国夫妇，我从心里感激他们。

小词典

陌生	mòshēng	形	strange; unfamiliar
路过	lùguò	动	pass by or through (a place)
名片	míngpiàn	名	name card
头重脚轻	tóuzhòng-jiǎoqīng		dizzy
汤面	tāngmiàn	名	noodles in soup
失约	shī yuē	动	fail to keep an appointment; break one's promise

专名

大连	Dàlián	Dalian

2. 回答下列问题 Answer the following questions

（1）作者是在什么地方学汉语的？

（2）他和饭店老板是怎么认识的？

（3）这个老板是个什么样的人？

（4）老板给他名片的时候，说了些什么话？

（5）他和饭店老板怎么成了朋友？

（6）他病的时候，老板怎么照顾他？

（7）他把自己的经历告诉朋友时，朋友相信吗？

（8）你遇到过让你印象很深的中国人吗？请给大家介绍一下。

3. 你是 A，请你向 B 提问 Supposing you are A, ask B questions

（1）A：____________________？（什么时候）

B：我是去年秋天到中国大连来学习中文的。

（2）A：____________________？（怎么样）

B：大连是个美丽的城市。可是，这里的一切对我来说，都是陌生的。

（3）A：____________________？（什么样）

B：饭店老板爱说爱笑，一看就觉得很亲切。

（4）A：____________________？（老板　什么）

B：老板对我说："你们学校离这里很近，你想吃什么就来吧，我们给你做。来不了的话，就打个电话，可以给你送过去。你离开家，到我们中国来不容易，要保重身体。吃好了，身体就好；身体好了，你父母也就放心了。"

（5）A：____________________？（怎么　成了）

B：后来我就经常去这家饭店吃饭。每次老板都会来到我身边，跟我聊一会儿。开始，我只能听他说，自己想说的话都说不出来。慢慢地我也能用汉语跟他们交流了，心里很高兴。就这样，我跟他们成了朋友。

（6）A：________________________？（老板　怎么）
B：一天，我感冒了，头重脚轻的，也不想吃东西。老板知道后，一连几天，都给我送来可口的饭菜。

（7）A：________________________？
（做什么　怎么了）
B：有一次，他说周末要开车带我出去玩儿，我答应了。可是出发的前一天，我的左手因为打球受伤了。

（8）A：________________________？（为什么）
B：我不想失约，所以还是跟他们去了。

（9）A：________________________？（朋友　吗）
B：我把自己的经历告诉了我的朋友，他不太相信。

（10）A：________________________？（怎么　喜欢上）
B：后来，朋友跟我一起去这个饭店吃饭，亲身感受到了他们的亲切和热情。他也喜欢上了这爱说爱笑的老板一家。

4. 请用作者的语气，讲讲这个故事 Tell this story in the author's tone

（八）朗读中国经典诗词，请注意语音语调 Read aloud the classic Chinese poem and pay attention to the pronunciation and intonation

Làngtáoshā
浪淘沙

[Táng] Liú Yǔxī
［唐］刘 禹锡（772—842）

Jiǔ qū Huáng Hé wàn lǐ shā, làng táo fēng bǒ zì tiānyá.
九曲黄河万里沙，浪淘风簸自天涯。
Rújīn zhí shàng yínhé qù, tóng dào Qiānniú Zhīnǚ jiā.
如今直上银河去，同到牵牛织女家。

（九）请欣赏下列著名的词句 Please enjoy the following famous saying

Shuǐ zhì qīng zé wú yú, rén zhì chá zé wú tú.

水至清则无鱼，人至察则无徒。

No fish can survive in the water if the water is too clean;

no one would like to make friends with someone who is too shrewd.

Dì-liùshíyī kè　　Jiàqī nǐ yǒu shénme dǎsuàn

第六十一课　假期你有什么打算

Lesson 61　What are your plans for the holiday?

一　课文 Text

A：快放假了，你有什么打算吗？

B：我去旅行，你呢？

A：我姐姐要结婚，我得回国去参加她的婚礼。你打算去什么地方？

B：我想先去西安，从西安去成都、重庆，再从重庆坐船游览长江三峡，到武汉下船，再去桂林和昆明，从昆明去香港，计划二十号左右回来。

A：你打算怎么去？

B：我想先坐高铁，去西安、成都和重庆，路上可以观赏铁路两边的风景；再坐轮船，观赏长江两岸的风光；之后再坐高铁去桂林和昆明；最后，坐飞机去香港。

A：你的想法不错，能充分享受大自然的美景。就你一个人去吗？

B：对。

A：为什么不跟旅行团一起去呢？

B：跟旅行团去比较受限制，不太自由。因为他们有固定的旅游路线，有可能你想去的地方，他们不去；他们要去的地方，你又不想去；到一个地方还没有仔细看呢，就催着快走。所以我决定自己去。

A：自己去好是好，但买火车票、船票、机票，找旅馆，也挺麻烦的。

B：是。不过，我想体验一下这种滋味，况且，我已经在网上预订了车票、船票、机票和旅馆。我想利用这个机会，练练自己的汉语。

A：最好找个旅伴，路上也好有个照应。

B：不太好找。

A：你可以在网上发个信息，说不定有人也正在找旅伴呢。

B：你这个办法倒不错，我可以试试，也许能行。如果有哪位同学愿意跟我一起去，就再好不过了。

二 生词 New Words

1	假期	jiàqī	名	vacation; holiday
2	打算	dǎsuàn	动、名	intend; plan; intention
3	放假	fàng jià	动	take a holiday
4	婚礼	hūnlǐ	名	wedding
5	游览	yóulǎn	动	go sightseeing; tour
6	计划	jìhuà	动、名	plan
7	观赏	guānshǎng	动	enjoy the sight of
8	铁路	tiělù	名	railway
9	岸	àn	名	bank; shore
10	充分	chōngfèn	形	full
11	旅行团	lǚxíngtuán	名	tour group
12	限制	xiànzhì	动、名	restrict; restriction
13	自由	zìyóu	形、名	free; freedom
14	固定	gùdìng	形、动	fixed; fix
15	旅游	lǚyóu	动	tour
16	路线	lùxiàn	名	itinerary
17	催	cuī	动	urge; hurry

18 决定	juédìng	动、名	decide; decision
19 票	piào	名	ticket
火车票	huǒchēpiào	名	railway ticket
船票	chuánpiào	名	steamer ticket; boat or ship ticket
机票	jīpiào	名	air ticket
20 旅馆	lǚguǎn	名	hotel
21 滋味	zīwèi	名	taste; experience; feeling
22 况且	kuàngqiě	连	besides
23 预订	yùdìng	动	book; reserve in advance
24 利用	lìyòng	动	make use of
25 旅伴	lǚbàn	名	traveling companion; fellow traveler
26 照应	zhàoyìng	动	look after; take care of

专名 Zhuānmíng Proper Nouns

1 成都	Chéngdū	Chengdu
2 重庆	Chóngqìng	Chongqing
3 武汉	Wǔhàn	Wuhan
5 长江三峡	Cháng Jiāng Sān Xiá	the Three Gorges of the Yangtze River
4 香港	Xiānggǎng	Hong Kong

三 注释 Notes

(一) 打算

“打算”既是动词又是名词。动词“打算”有计划、考虑、准备等意思，在句中做谓语，可以带宾语。例如：

“打算” is both a verb and a noun. When used as a verb, it means “to plan, consider, or prepare”.

It is used as a predicate and is followed by an object. For example:

1. 大学毕业后我打算考研究生。
2. 寒假我打算去南方旅行。
3. 你打算不打算买辆电动车？

名词"打算"可以做宾语，例如：

When used as a noun, "打算" can be used as an object. For example:

1. 这个假期你有什么打算？
2. 为了以后能找到好工作，要早做打算。

（二）先……然后……再／又……

"先……然后……再……"用来叙述将要实施的行为计划和程序。"先……然后……又……"叙述已完成的动作行为的历程。例如：

"先……然后……再……" is used to describe the plan and procedures of an action to be implemented. "先……然后……又……" is used to describe the process of an action that has been completed. For example:

1. 我先去西安，然后从西安去成都和重庆，再从重庆坐船游览一下长江三峡，到武汉下船，再从武汉去桂林、昆明。
2. 明天我先去教室上课，然后做练习，下午再去学习拉二胡。（明天的行动）
3. 昨天我先上的汉语课，然后做作业，又去上了两个钟头的书画课。（昨天已经完成的动作行为）

（三）左右

名词"左右"用在数量词后面表示概数。例如：

The noun "左右" is used after a quantifier to indicate an approximate number. For example:

1. 我计划二十号左右回来。
2. 我每天十点左右睡觉。
3. 他们班的学生有二十个左右。
4. 这种手机两千元左右。

（四）况且

连词“况且”表示在已经有的理由之外，再追加另外的理由。例如：

The conjunction “况且” means “to add another reason to the existing one”. For example:

1. 我不太愿意参加中学同学聚会。因为大家多年不见，都不认识了，况且，见面说什么呀？
2. 我现在很少用电脑，都是用手机，手机功能齐全，况且携带也方便。

（五）也许

副词“也许”表示估计、猜测和不太肯定。在句中放在动词或形容词前面做状语，也可以用在主语前面。例如：

The adverb “也许” indicates estimation, speculation and uncertainty. It is put before a verb or an adjective in a sentence as an adverbial. It can also be used before a subject. For example:

1. 你看这天，也许要下雨。
2. 他到现在还没来，也许是有什么事了。
3. 你试一试，也许能行。
4. 从这儿走也许近一点儿。

四 练习 Exercises

（一）朗读 Read aloud

1. 朗读下列发音相近的词语 Read the following words with similar pronunciation

xiànzhì 限制	xiānzhī 先知	zìyóu 自由	zhìyǒu 挚友
yùdìng 预订	yídìng 一定	yóulǎn 游览	yǒngyuǎn 永远
jīhuì 机会	jìhuì 忌讳	guānshǎng 观赏	guānshang 关上

2. 朗读下列短语 Read the following phrases aloud

受：受限制　受气　受委屈　受教育　受表扬　受批评

自由：自由参加　自由安排　自由自在　自由发言
滋味：想家的滋味　孤独的滋味　寂寞的滋味
　　　体验单独旅行的滋味
照应：互相照应　彼此照应　前后照应　有个照应

（二）**替换并朗读** Replace and read aloud

1. 快放寒假了，你有什么打算？

| 放暑假 | 圣诞节 |
| 春节 | 毕业 |

2. 我朋友要结婚，我得回国参加她/他的婚礼。

| 姐姐 | 妹妹 | 哥哥 | 弟弟 |

3. 你打算怎么去？

| 来 | 做 | 练 | 写 | 说 |

4. 我想坐高铁去。

| 坐飞机 | 坐船 | 开车 |
| 打的 | 骑车 | |

（三）**选词填空并朗读下列句子** Choose the appropriate words to fill in the blanks and read aloud the following sentences

| 风光 | 照应 | 打算 | 就 | 机会 | 再 |

1. A：快放假了，你有什么________？
   B：我打算去旅行。
2. 我想先去西安，从西安去成都、重庆，________从重庆坐船游览长江三峡，到武汉下船，再去桂林和昆明，从昆明去香港，计划二十号左右回来。

3. A：你怎么去？
   B：我想先坐高铁，去西安、成都和重庆，路上可以观赏铁路两边的风景，再坐轮船，观赏长江两岸的________。
4. 你的想法不错，能充分享受大自然的美景。________你一个人去吗？
5. 我想体验一下这种滋味，况且，我已经在网上预订了车票、船票、机票和旅馆。我是想利用这个________，练练自己的汉语。
6. 你最好找个旅伴，路上也好有个________。

寂寞　决定　滋味　跟　旅游　催

1. 你这次的________路线非常好。
2. 我觉得________旅行团去比较好，买票、住旅馆、吃饭等都由他们办，不管到哪儿去，还有车接车送，非常好。
3. ________他快点儿，车在外边等着呢。
4. 这个假期我________去西藏看看，听说那是个神奇的地方。
5. 你没有体验过一个人在国外生活的________吧，这次你可以体验体验了。
6. 还是两个人一起去旅行比较好，可以互相照应，也不________。

（四）请用“先……然后……再／又……”说一段话 Please compose a paragraph with “先……然后……再／又……”

1. 昨天早上，我先________________，然后________________，又________________。
2. 明天星期六，我跟朋友商量好了。我们先________________，然后________________，再________________。
3. 我想去中国南方旅行，打算先________________，然后________________，再________________，最后从________________回来。
4. 我的人生计划是，来中国以后，先________________，然后________________，再________________，将来当一名________________。

（五）完成下列句子并大声朗读 Complete the following sentences and read them aloud

1. ________________，要不要把室内的温度调高点儿？（也许）
2. 他没跟你打招呼，________________，你不必在意。（也许）
3. 她这么说，你________________，但她真是一片好心。（也许）
4. ________________，不然不会一见你就脸红。（也许）
5. 你这次一出国________________，我怎么办？你想过吗？（也许）
6. 你________________有人也在找旅伴呢。（也许）
7. 天已经晚了，________________，明天再说吧。（况且）
8. 咱们还是坐地铁去吧，地铁准时，________________。（况且）

（六）完成下列会话并大声朗读 Complete the following conversations and read them aloud

1. A：______________________________________？
（打算　计划　准备）
B：假期我想去旅行。
2. A：______________________________________？
（哪儿　旅行路线）
B：我先去西安，然后从西安去成都和重庆，再从重庆坐船游览一下长江三峡，到武汉下船，再从武汉去桂林、昆明，从昆明去香港。
3. A：你打算怎么去？
B：______________________________________。
（自己一个人　坐火车　飞机）
4. A：______________________________________？
（为什么　跟……一起去）
B：跟旅行团受限制，不太自由，到一个地方还没有仔细看呢，就催你快走。

5. A：自己旅游好是好，可是买火车票、船票、机票，找旅馆都很不方便。

B：____。

（想　体验　练　口语）

6. A：最好找个旅伴，两个人路上也有个照应。你可以在网上发个信息看能不能找到旅伴，也许有人也在找旅伴呢。

B：____。

（试试　说不定）

（七）和同学一起表演课文 Act out the text with your classmates

（八）自由表达 Express yourself freely

和同学一起说说自己的假期计划：假期准备做什么？旅行、回国，还是待在学校里？旅行准备去哪里？怎么去？去多长时间？为什么要回国？回多长时间？等等。

（九）读后说 Read the passage and say it

1. 朗读 Read aloud

滴水之恩

南山寺的住持法一大师突然得了重病，请了许多大夫，用了好多药都不见好。后来一位大夫建议："试试山红花这种药吧。"

山红花是一种名贵的药材，需要每年春天带着花一起采摘。据说南山寺后面的南山里就有，但是生长在悬崖峭壁上，数量很少，很难采摘。

一位药农听说此事后，就把自己珍藏的一棵山红花送给了大师。大师服用后，病奇迹般地好了。

来年春天，法一大师开始让寺里的徒弟上山采药。这些徒弟个个年轻力壮，有的还有一身好功夫，所以每年总能采摘到一两棵山红花。大师每年都精心挑选一棵送给那个药农。

转眼九年过去了。寺里并不宽裕，好多徒弟对大师的做法很不理解。用一棵还一棵就可以了，哪有年年给的道理？

这天，大师问大家：“我们给了送药的施主几棵山红花了？”

徒弟们异口同声地说：“九棵了。”只有一个叫可慧的徒弟不开口。大师便专门问他，他说：“一棵。”

大师又问他：“为什么是一棵？”

可慧说：“没有一哪来九！”

其他徒弟恍然大悟。大师认为可慧能悟出“滴水之恩，当涌泉相报”的道理，便将住持的位子传给了他。

再贵的东西都无法和生命相比。真善无价，只是有人总喜欢把它折合成金钱。

小词典

住持	zhùchí	名、动	(Buddhist or Taoist) abbot
大师	dàshī	名	master
名贵	míngguì	形	rare; precious
药材	yàocái	名	medicinal material
采摘	cǎizhāi	动	pick; pluck
悬崖峭壁	xuányá-qiàobì		precipice; cliff
药农	yàonóng	名	herb farmer; herb collector
珍藏	zhēncáng	动、名	treasure up; rare and valuable articles collected and treasured up
奇迹	qíjì	名	miracle
精心	jīngxīn	形	careful; meticulous
挑选	tiāoxuǎn	动	select
宽裕	kuānyù	形	well-to-do
道理	dàolǐ	名	truth; principle; reason
施主	shīzhǔ	名	(monks or priests' form of address for) those who give money or food to the monastery or Taoist temple

异口同声	yìkǒu-tóngshēng		with one voice; in unison
专门	zhuānmén	副	specially
恍然大悟	huǎngrán-dàwù		realize all of a sudden; suddenly see the light
悟	wù	动	understand; comprehend
滴水之恩，当涌泉相报	dī shuǐ zhī ēn, dāng yǒng quán xiāng bào		Receive drips of water when in need, and return the kindness with a spring.
无价	wújià	动	priceless
折合	zhéhé	动	convert into

专名

南山寺	Nánshān Sì	Nanshan Temple
法一	Fǎyī	name of a person
可慧	Kěhuì	name of a person

2. 回答下列问题 Answer the questions

（1）法一大师怎么了？

（2）大夫建议他吃什么药？

（3）这种药材容易得到吗？

（4）谁给了法一大师一棵山红花？

（5）大师吃了这种药以后病好了没有？

（6）大师是怎么感谢这位药农的？

（7）徒弟们对大师这样做有什么看法？

（8）大师为什么把住持的位子传给了徒弟可慧？

（9）“滴水之恩，当涌泉相报”是什么意思？

3. 你是 A，请你向 B 提问 Supposing you are A, ask B questions

（1）A: ________________________？（怎么了）

B：南山寺的住持法一大师得了重病。

（2）A：______________________________？

（什么　药）

B：后来一位大夫建议试试山红花。

（3）A：______________________________？

（容易　不容易）

B：不容易。这是一种名贵的药材，生长在悬崖峭壁上，数量极少，很难采摘。

（4）A：______________________________？（谁）

B：一位药农听说此事后，就把自己珍藏的一棵山红花送给了法一大师。大师服用后，病奇迹般地好了。

（5）A：______________________________？

（怎么　报答）

B：来年春天，法一大师开始让寺里的徒弟上山采药。这些徒弟个个年轻力壮，有的还有一身好功夫，所以每年总能采摘到一两棵山红花。大师每年都挑选一棵送给那个药农。

（6）A：______________________________？

（徒弟　怎么）

B：寺里并不宽裕，好多徒弟对大师的做法不理解，认为用一棵还一棵就可以了，哪有年年给的道理？

（7）A：______________________________？

（当大师问……时　谁）

B：当大师问："我们给了送药的施主几棵药材了？"的时候，徒弟们异口同声地说："九棵。"只有一个叫可慧的徒弟不开口。大师专门问这个徒弟，他说："一棵。"

（8）A：______________________________？

（为什么　传）

B：因为大师认为可慧懂得"滴水之恩，当涌泉相报"的道理，就将住持的位子传给了可慧。

4. 复述这篇课文 Retell this text

（十）朗读中国经典诗词，请注意语音语调 Read aloud the classic Chinese poem and pay attention to the pronunciation and intonation

Xiǎo Chū Jìngcí Sì Sòng Lín Zǐfāng
晓 出 净慈 寺 送 林 子方

[Sòng] Yáng Wànlǐ
［宋］ 杨 万里（1127—1206）

Bìjìng Xī Hú Liùyuè zhōng, fēngguāng bù yǔ sìshí tóng.
毕竟 西 湖 六月 中， 风光 不与 四时 同。
Jiē tiān liányè wúqióng bì, yìng rì héhuā biéyàng hóng.
接 天 莲叶 无穷 碧， 映 日 荷花 别样 红。

（十一）请欣赏下列著名的词句 Please enjoy the following famous saying

Xué ér bú yàn, huì rén bú juàn.
学 而 不 厌， 诲 人 不 倦。

Be insatiable in learning and tireless in teaching others.

Dì-liùshí'èr kè Wǒ cānguānle bīngmǎyǒng

第六十二课 我参观了兵马俑

Lesson 62 I visited the terracotta warriors and horses

一 课文 Text

（一）我参观了兵马俑

（假期过后，同学们旅行回来了……）

老 师：同学们假期都去哪儿了？

罗 兰：我去云南了。

老 师：怎么样？

罗 兰：云南的风光太迷人了。尤其是丽江、玉龙雪山，真是如诗如画。因为我对少数民族的风俗很感兴趣，本来还打算去别的地方，但是到了云南就哪儿也不想去了，所以在那儿一待就是一个星期。

安 丽：我去爬泰山了，在泰山上看了日出，非常壮观。

老 师：你呢，爱德华？你去哪儿了？

爱德华：这个假期，我因为腿受伤了，哪儿也没去。

麦 克：老师，我去西安了。

老 师：都参观了什么地方？

麦 克：我参观了碑林、华清池，还看了看秦始皇的警察。

老 师：那叫兵马俑。

麦 克：对！是兵马俑，我总记不住这个词。我觉得最有意思的还是兵马俑。我还带回来一个。看！这就是小兵马俑。

罗 兰：这是兵马俑的纪念品吧？以前我看过一个电影，就是关于兵马俑的，特有意思，可我一直没机会去西安看看。

麦 克：以后有机会去西安看看吧。

（二）黄山归来不看岳

玛　丽：丹尼丝，听说你去哈尔滨看冰灯了，什么时候回来的？

丹尼丝：昨天晚上。

玛　丽：怎么样？

丹尼丝：哈尔滨的冰灯、冰雕漂亮极了，到了那儿，简直像走进了童话世界。对了，玛丽，你去哪儿旅行了？

玛　丽：我去了一趟黄山。

丹尼丝：黄山怎么样？

玛　丽：好极了。中国同学说，五岳归来不看山，黄山归来不看岳。不去不知道，去了一看，一点儿也不假。黄山太美了！你看看我拍的这些照片就知道了。

丹尼丝：这是什么地方？

玛　丽：这就是飞来峰，这块大石头，好像从天上飞来的一样，所以叫飞来峰。

丹尼丝：真奇妙！

玛　丽：黄山有四大景观：奇松、怪石、温泉、云海。你看，这是迎客松；这是云海，云海千变万化，美不胜收。

丹尼丝：真好，这一幅幅照片真比山水画还好看。你是一个人去的吗？

玛　丽：不是，我是跟旅行团去的。我觉得自己去太麻烦，旅行团管买票，去哪儿都车接车送，还有导游跟着，比较省心。我建议你也去看看吧，如果来中国一次，连黄山都没去过，那简直太遗憾了。

丹尼丝：中国可游玩的山水太多了，哪儿能都去呀？

玛　丽：那倒也是。

二 生词 New Words

1	兵马俑	bīngmǎyǒng	名	terracotta warriors and horses
2	风光	fēngguāng	名	landscape
3	迷人	mírén	形	enchanting; charming
4	如诗如画	rúshī-rúhuà		picturesque
	如	rú	动	like; as if
	诗	shī	名	poetry; poem
5	日出	rìchū	动	sunrise
6	壮观	zhuàngguān	形、名	magnificent; grand sight
7	碑林	bēilín	名	forest of steles
8	纪念品	jìniànpǐn	名	souvenir
	纪念	jìniàn	动、名	commemorate; commemoration
9	冰灯	bīngdēng	名	ice lantern
10	冰雕	bīngdiāo	名	ice sculpture
11	童话	tónghuà	名	fairy tale
12	岳	yuè		high mountain
13	归	guī	动	return; go or come back
14	景观	jǐngguān	名	landscape
15	奇	qí		strange
16	松	sōng	名	pine (tree)
17	温泉	wēnquán	名	hot spring
18	云海	yúnhǎi	名	sea of clouds
19	千变万化	qiānbiàn-wànhuà		ever-changing
20	美不胜收	měibúshèngshōu		there are more beautiful things than the eyes can take in

21 管	guǎn	动	be in charge of
22 导游	dǎoyóu	动、名	guide; tour guide service; tour guide
23 省心	shěng xīn	动	free from worry or anxiety

专名 Zhuānmíng Proper Nouns

1 云南	Yúnnán	Yunnan
2 丽江	Lìjiāng	Lijiang
3 玉龙雪山	Yùlóng Xuěshān	Yulong Snow Mountain
4 华清池	Huáqīng Chí	Huaqingchi
5 黄山	Huáng Shān	Mount Huang
6 秦始皇	Qín Shǐhuáng	Qinshihuang, the first emperor of China

三 注释 Notes

(一) 如

好像，如同。常用于熟语和四字格。例如：

"如" means "as if", "like". It is often used in idioms and four-character expressions. For example:

1. 云南的山水如诗如画。
2. 我们班十八个同学来自十三个国家，大家在一起亲如一家。
3. 学习如逆水行舟，不进则退（nìshuǐ-xíngzhōu, bújìn-zétuì, a boat sailing against the current must forge ahead, or it will be driven back）。我两个星期没来上课，就觉得跟不上了。

(二) 形容词 + 极了

"极了"常用在形容词后边做补语。"形容词 + 极了"的意思是：非常 / 很 + 形容词，例如：

"极了" is often used as a complement after an adjective. "Adjective + 极了" means "very/quite + adjective". For example：

1. 哈尔滨的冰灯冰雕漂亮极了，到了那儿，简直像走进了童话世界。
2. 我最近又要准备比赛又要准备考试，忙极了。
3. 昨天的电影好看极了，你没去看真是太遗憾了。
4. 我去过一次哈尔滨，那儿的冬天冷极了。

（三）五岳归来不看山，黄山归来不看岳

这是一句俗语。意思是：如果你去看了五岳，那么回来以后，就不用看别的山了（别的山都没有五岳美）；但是，你要是去看了黄山，那你连五岳都不用看了（黄山比五岳更美）。

五岳是中国五大名山的总称，即东岳泰山、南岳衡山、西岳华山、北岳恒山、中岳嵩山。

This is a popular saying, meaning if you've been to *Wuyue* (or the Five Mountains), you don't need to see other mountains after you come back (since none of them is as beautiful as *Wuyue*). However, if you've been to Mount Huang, you don't even need to see *Wuyue* (since Mount Huang is more beautiful than these mountains).

"*Wuyue*" is the generic term for the five famous Chinese mountains, namely Mount Tai in the east, Mount Heng in the south, Mount Hua in the west, Mount Heng in the north and Mount Song in the middle.

四 练习 Exercises

（一）朗读 Read aloud

1. 朗读下列发音相近的词语 Read aloud the following words with similar pronunciation

zhuàngguān 壮观	zhuān guǎn 专　管	shítou 石头	shìtou 势头

jǐngguān 景观	jīngguǎn 经管	wēnquán 温泉	wènjuàn 问卷
shěng xīn 省 心	shēnxìn 深信	tónghuà 童话	dònghuà 动画

2. 朗读下列短语 Read the following phrases aloud

如：如诗如画　如饥似渴　如鱼得水　如影随形　如梦初醒

日出：海上日出　泰山日出　东方日出　观看日出　日出的景色

一……就……：一待就是一个星期　一坐就是一个上午

一去就一年　一玩儿就是半天

一学就是两三个小时

（二）替换并朗读 Replace and read aloud

1. 我在泰山上看了日出，非常壮观。

海边　船上
草原上　山顶上
飞机上

2. 我对少数民族的风俗很感兴趣。

中国的文化
中国民族音乐
少数民族的歌舞
中国的历史
中国功夫
中医

3. 我因为腿受伤了，所以哪儿也没去。

生病了	没有参加活动
要参加国内大学的考试	得回国
手机没电了	没有给你回信
路上堵车	来晚了

4. 如果来中国一次，连黄山都没去过，那简直太遗憾了。

长城	桂林	杭州
上海	西安	西藏
新疆		

（三）**选词填空并朗读下列句子** Choose the appropriate words to fill in the blanks and read aloud the following sentences

壮观　也　还　住　尤其　就是

1. 云南的风光太迷人了。________是丽江、玉龙雪山，真是如诗如画。
2. 因为我对少数民族的风俗很感兴趣，本来还打算去别的地方，但是到了云南就哪儿也不想去了，所以我在那儿一待________一个星期。
3. 我去爬泰山了，在泰山顶上看了日出，非常________。
4. 这个假期，我因为腿受伤了，哪儿________没去。
5. A：我参观了碑林、华清池，________看了看秦始皇的警察。
   B：是兵马俑。
6. 对！是兵马俑，我总记不________这个词。我觉得最有意思的还是兵马俑。

遗憾　来　趟　景观　假　世界

1. 哈尔滨的冰灯、冰雕漂亮极了，到了那儿，简直像走进了童话________。
2. A：玛丽，你去哪儿旅行了？
   B：我去了一________黄山。
3. 中国人说，五岳归来不看山，黄山归来不看岳。不去不知道，去了一看，一点儿也不________。黄山太美了！你看看我拍的这些照片就知道了。

4. 这就是飞来峰，这块大石头，好像从天上飞________的一样，所以叫飞来峰。
5. 黄山有四大________：奇松、怪石、温泉、云海。你看，这是迎客松；这是云海，云海千变万化，美不胜收。
6. 我建议你也去看看吧，如果来中国一次，连黄山都没去过，那简直太________了。

极了　画　省心　美不胜收　日出　壮观

1. 我去过杭州的西湖，那如诗如________的风景让我难忘。
2. 去泰山旅行的旅客都希望看到________。
3. 站在黄山山顶看云海，千变万化，非常________。
4. 哈尔滨的冰灯、冰雕真是漂亮________。
5. 如果你有机会到桂林，你就知道，桂林的山水真是________。
6. 我想跟旅行团一起去，因为跟他们去比较________。

（四）完成下列句子并大声朗读 Complete the following sentences and read them aloud

1. 这个假期我____________________，后来她要我跟她一起去旅行，所以，我就没有回去。（本来）
2. 我本来也住留学生公寓，为了____________________。（就）
3. 在我感到孤独的时候，她像姐姐一样，对我____________________。（特别）
4. 学汉语是我自己的选择，所以____________________。（一直）
5. 昨天的作业比较多，所以____________________。（一直）
6. 对我来说，学习汉语真的不容易，____________________。（尤其是）

（五）完成下列会话并大声朗读 Complete the following conversations and read them aloud

1. A：罗兰，你去哪儿旅行了？
   B：______________________________。（云南）

2. A：你觉得云南怎么样？

B：____。

（迷人　尤其是　如诗如画）

3. A：丹尼丝，你去哪儿了？

B：____。

（哈尔滨　冰灯　冰雕）

4. A：你觉得黄山怎么样？

B：____。

（美　千变万化　美不胜收）

5. A：黄山有哪四大景观？

B：____。

（奇松　怪石　温泉　云海）

6. A：你是一个人去的吗？

B：____。

（不是　麻烦　旅行团　管　省心）

（六）和同学一起表演课文 Act out the text with your classmates

（七）自由表达 Express yourself freely

和同学互相介绍一下你们来中国后的旅行经历：去过什么地方？那里的风景怎么样？遇到过什么有趣的事情？认识了什么人？

（八）读后说 Read the passage and say it

1. 朗读 Read aloud

放飞蝴蝶

一天早晨，我到学校办公室刚坐下，便有人对我说，我们班教室里有两块窗玻璃在昨晚被风刮破了。我马上回到教室，看看是怎么回事。

我找来昨天的值日生丁兰。她有点儿害怕地说："昨晚放学时，教室里飞进来两只蝴蝶，赶来赶去，总有一只飞不出去。我只好开着一扇窗户，好让外面那只飞进来，或者里面这只飞出去，让它们结伴儿去玩儿。

没想到晚上刮大风，打破了玻璃……”小女孩儿几乎要落泪，她说愿意赔这两块玻璃的钱。

听了孩子的话，我又感动又高兴。感动的是，孩子爱护生命、呵护生命的那颗爱心；高兴的是，自己平时对学生们的教导，孩子们正在身体力行。于是，我抚摸着她的头，对她说："好孩子，你做得对！玻璃不用你赔，快去玩儿吧。"

后来我去了学校财务室，对他们说："请在我下个月的工资中扣除那两块玻璃的钱。"没想到，校长知道这件事后，为了鼓励学生爱护生命的行为，并没有让我赔玻璃的钱。

我回到教室一看，新的窗户玻璃已经被工人师傅安好了。

小词典

放飞	fàngfēi	动	set free; free
飞	fēi	动	fly
蝴蝶	húdié	名	butterfly
玻璃	bōli	名	glass
值日	zhírì	动	be on duty
害怕	hài pà	动	fear; afraid
扇	shàn	量、名	*a measure word for windows, doors, etc.*; fan
结伴儿	jié bànr	动	go with
呵护	hēhù	动	take good care of
教导	jiàodǎo	动	teach
身体力行	shēntǐ-lìxíng		earnestly practice what one advocates or preaches
抚摸	fǔmō	动	caress; stroke
赔	péi	动	compensate for
财务	cáiwù	名	finance
扣除	kòuchú	动	deduct

2. 回答下列问题 Answer the following questions

（1）“我”到学校办公室刚坐下，就听到了什么消息？

（2）教室的玻璃是怎么破的？

（3）值日生丁兰的心情怎么样？

（4）“我”听了丁兰的话为什么又感动又高兴？

（5）最后“我”赔玻璃的钱了吗？

3. 你是 A，请你向 B 提问 Supposing you are A, ask B questions

（1）A：________________________________？

（发生　什么　事）

B：早晨，我到学校办公室刚坐下，便有人对我说，我们班教室里有两块窗玻璃在昨晚被风刮破了。

（2）A：________________________________？

（玻璃　怎么　破）

B：我找来昨天的值日生丁兰。她有点儿害怕地说：“昨晚放学时，教室里有两只蝴蝶，赶来赶去，总有一只飞不出教室。我只好开着一扇窗户，好让外面的那只飞进来，或者里面的这只飞出去，让它们结伴儿去玩儿。没想到会被大风刮破了玻璃……”

（3）A：________________________________？

（丁兰　什么）

B：丁兰几乎要落泪，她说愿意赔这两块玻璃的钱。

（4）A：________________________________？

（听了孩子的话　为什么　又……又……）

B：感动的是，孩子爱护生命、呵护生命的那颗爱心；高兴的是，自己平时对学生们的教导，孩子们正在身体力行。

（5）A：________________________________？（你　什么）

B：我摸了摸她的头，对她说：“好孩子，做得对！玻璃不用你赔，快去玩儿吧。”

（6）A: ________________________________？（赔）

B: 我想赔这两块玻璃的钱，可校长知道这件事后，为了鼓励学生爱护生命的行为，没有让我赔玻璃的钱。

4. 复述这篇课文 Retell this text

（九）朗读中国经典诗词，请注意语音语调 Read aloud the classic Chinese poem and pay attention to the pronunciation and intonation

Zǎo Chūn
早 春

[Táng] Hán Yù
［唐］韩 愈（768—824）

Tiān jiē xiǎoyǔ rùn rú sū, cǎo sè yáo kàn jìn què wú.
天街小雨润如酥，草色遥看近却无。
Zuì shì yì nián chūn hǎo chù, jué shèng yān liǔ mǎn huángdū.
最是一年春好处，绝胜烟柳满皇都。

（十）请欣赏下列著名的词句 Please enjoy the following famous saying

Dé dào duō zhù, shī dào guǎ zhù.
得道多助，失道寡助。

A just cause enjoys abundant support, while an unjust one finds little.

Dì-liùshísān kè　Gào bié shī yǒu

第六十三课　告别师友

Lesson 63　Say goodbye to teachers and friends

一 课文 Text

（一）祝你一路平安

（就要回国了，留学生黄春燕向老师告别，跟老师语音通话……）

黄春燕：老师，我是黄春燕，我想去看看您，不知道您现在方便不方便？

老　师：好，你来吧。

（在老师家）

黄春燕：老师，我后天就要回国了。

老　师：是吗？时间过得真快，不知不觉地，都到你该回国的时间了。你回去后打算做什么？

黄春燕：当幼儿教师。初步打算是办一个幼儿园，教孩子们认字、唱歌、跳舞什么的。

老　师：啊？你什么时候产生这个想法的？

黄春燕：早就有了，因为我特别喜欢孩子。

老　师：我想起来了，你是师范大学教育系学前教育专业毕业的。

黄春燕：是。

老　师：难怪。那以后我们就是同行了。

黄春燕：哪里。我虽然跟老师学习的时间很短，只有一年，但这一年留学的经历却使我终生难忘。这段时间，不仅提高了我的汉语水平，更重要的是，我还学会了许多书本上学不到的东西。不但增长了知识，也增长了见识，更增强了我学好汉语和独立生活的信心。

老　师：老师从同学们身上也学到了很多东西，教学相长嘛。和你们在一起，老师感到非常快乐。回去以后常联系吧，需要帮助的话，就发微信。只要能做到的，老师一定帮你。

黄春燕：谢谢老师。那我就告辞了，老师多保重。

老　师：祝你一路平安。

（二）真舍不得你走

（黄春燕是班长，同学们都叫她“大姐”。她来向小玉和青木告别……）

黄春燕：小玉、青木，你们都在呀，我明天就要走了。

小　玉：真的吗？这么快！大姐，我真舍不得你走。

黄春燕：我也舍不得呀。我舍不得离开你们，也舍不得离开我们的老师和学校。

小　玉：不知不觉我们在一起学习已经一年了，我们班真像个大家庭一样。

黄春燕：是呀，我们遇到了好老师，也遇到了好同学。我总想，在中国留学的这一年，我会记一辈子的。

青　木：我也是。你去看老师了吗？

黄春燕：去了，昨天去的。

小　玉：大姐，你们都要走了，只有我和青木留下来，不知道什么时候咱们能再见面呢？

黄春燕：我们还会见面的。

青　木：我们不是都有大姐的微信吗？我们可以跟她在网上聊天儿呀。

小　玉：那还是不一样啊！我希望大家以后常来中国，我们再见面，还在老师家里聚会。大家一起包饺子、炸春卷儿，一起吃火锅，喝老师给我们泡的茶……

（小玉说着说着就掉眼泪了）

黄春燕：好了，别哭了，我一定再回来。等你们俩把本科读完，把学士学位拿下来时，我们班同学一起来为你们庆贺，怎么样？

小　玉：好啊。大姐，一言为定，你们一定要来呀。

黄春燕：咱们说好了，一定！

二 生词 New Words

1	告别	gào bié	动	say goodbye
2	幼儿	yòu'ér	名	child
	幼儿园	yòu'éryuán	名	kindergarten; nursery school
3	教师	jiàoshī	名	teacher
4	初步	chūbù	形	preliminary; initial
5	认	rèn	动	learn to read; recognize
6	师范	shīfàn	名	normal school
7	教育	jiàoyù	动、名	educate; education
8	学前教育	xuéqián-jiàoyù		preschool education
9	同行	tóngháng	名	peer; counterpart
10	终生	zhōngshēng	名	all one's life
11	不仅	bùjǐn	连	not only
12	增长	zēngzhǎng	动	increase; rise
13	独立	dúlì	动	do sth. on one's own
14	教学相长	jiàoxué-xiāngzhǎng		mutual advance between teaching and studying
15	告辞	gàocí	动	bid farewell; say goodbye (to sb.)
16	保重	bǎozhòng	动	take care of
17	一辈子	yíbèizi	名	all one's life
18	见面	jiàn miàn	动	meet; see

19 炸	zhá	动	fry
20 春卷儿	chūnjuǎnr	名	spring roll (a thin sheet of dough, rolled, stuffed, and fried)
21 泡	pào	动、名	make (tea); bubble
22 掉	diào	动	shed; fall
23 眼泪	yǎnlèi	名	tear
24 本科	běnkē	名	regular college course; undergraduate course
25 学士	xuéshì	名	bachelor
26 学位	xuéwèi	名	academic degree
27 一言为定	yìyánwéidìng		It's a deal.

专名 Zhuānmíng Proper Nouns

1 黄春燕	Huáng Chūnyàn	name of a person
2 小玉	Xiǎoyù	name of a person
3 青木	Qīngmù	name of a person

三 注释 Notes

(一) ……什么的

"什么的"用在一个成分或并列的几个成分之后，表示"等等"的意思。例如：

"什么的" is used after one or several parallel elements to mean "and so on" or "things like that". For example:

1. 我喜欢吃巧克力、饼干、冰激凌什么的。
2. 我想把这些钥匙链、玩偶、贴纸什么的当礼物送人。
3. 杂志、图书、画册什么的，堆了一桌子。

（二）不仅

“不仅”是“不只是，不但”的意思，可以与“而且、并且”连用，表示除了所说的意思之外，还有更进一层的意思。例如：

“不仅” means “not only”. It can be used together with “而且” or “并且” to indicate that in addition to what was said, it has a further meaning. For example:

1. 老师的教育使我终生难忘，不仅提高了我的汉语水平，更重要的是，让我学会了许多书本上学不到的东西。
2. 来中国留学不仅要学习语言，而且还要了解中国，了解中国的文化。
3. 他不仅是我们的老师，并且也是我们的朋友。

（三）舍不得

“舍不得”表示说话人对某人和某地有感情，不愿离开；对东西爱惜，不愿意使用。反义词是“舍得”。例如：

“舍不得” means that the speaker has feelings towards someone or some place and is reluctant to leave, or the speaker cherishes something so much that he does not want to use it. Its antonym is “舍得”. For example:

1. 我舍不得离开你们，也舍不得离开我们的老师和学校。
2. 大姐，我真舍不得你走。
3. 这些点心妈妈舍不得吃，都给你留着呢。

四 练习 Exercises

（一）朗读 Read aloud

1. 朗读下列发音相近的词语 Read aloud the following words with similar pronunciation

jiàoyù	jiāoyì	xuéwèi	xuéhuì
教育	交易	学位	学会

shīfàn	shìfàn	zhōngshēng	zhōngshēn
师范	示范	终生	终身
zēngzhǎng	zēngqiáng	jùhuì	jīhuì
增长	增强	聚会	机会

2. 朗读下列短语 Read the following phrases aloud

告别：告别家乡　告别亲人　告别朋友　告别老师　告别母校

初步：初步打算　初步计划　初步考虑　初步决定　初步建议

专业：语言专业　文学专业　历史专业　外贸专业　特教专业

教育：学前教育　成人教育　大学教育　家庭教育　高等教育

系：外语系　中文系　历史系　外贸系　计算机系

保重：请多保重　多加保重　保重身体

舍不得：舍不得用　舍不得吃　舍不得离开　舍不得妈妈　舍不得同学　舍不得离开家

炸：炸春卷儿　炸馒头（mántou, steamed bread）　炸薯片儿（shǔpiànr, potato chips）　炸鱼

学位：学士学位　硕士（shuòshì, master's）学位　博士（bóshì, doctor's）学位

（二）替换并朗读 Replace and read aloud

1. 你回国以后打算做什么？

> 毕业以后　这个周末　寒假
> 暑假　今天晚上

2. 我想当幼儿教师。

> 汉语教师　体育记者　翻译
> 外交官　律师　志愿者

3. A：你在大学时是学什么专业的？
   B：我是<u>学前教育</u>专业毕业的。

中医	汉语	文学
特教	外贸	历史

4. 等你们俩把<u>学士学位</u>拿下来时，
   我们一起来为你们庆贺，怎么样？

硕士学位	博士学位
毕业证书	HSK 高级证书

（三）**选词填空并朗读下列句子** Choose the appropriate words to fill in the blanks and read aloud the following sentences

起来　该　到　不　的话　什么的

1. 老师，我是黄春燕，我想去看看您，不知道您现在方便________方便？
2. 时间过得真快，不知不觉地，都到你________回国的时间了。你回去后打算做什么？
3. 当幼儿教师。初步打算是办一个幼儿园，教孩子们认字、唱歌、跳舞________。
4. 我想________了，你是师范大学教育系学前教育专业毕业的。
5. 这一年的学习不仅提高了我的汉语水平，更重要的是，我还学会了许多书本上学不________的东西，增强了学好汉语和独立生活的信心。
6. 和你们在一起，老师感到非常快乐。回去以后常联系吧，需要帮助________，就发微信。只要能做到的，老师一定帮你。

下来　不觉　舍　给　记　定　离开　再

1. A：小玉、青木，你们都在呀，我明天就要走了。
   B：真的吗？这么快！大姐，我真________不得你走。

2. 我也舍不得呀。我舍不得________你们，也舍不得________我们的老师和学校。
3. 不知________我们在一起学习已经一年了，我们班真像个大家庭一样。
4. 是呀，我们遇到了好老师，也遇到了好同学。我总想，在中国留学的这一年，我会________一辈子的。
5. 大姐，你们都要走了，只有我和青木留下来，不知道什么时候咱们能________见面呢？
6. 我希望大家以后常来中国，我们再见面，还在老师家里聚会。大家一起包饺子、炸春卷儿，一起吃火锅，喝老师________我们泡的茶……
7. 好了，别哭了，我一定再回来。等你们俩把本科读完，把学士学位拿________时，我们班同学一起来为你们庆贺，怎么样？
8. 好啊。大姐，一言为________，你们一定要来呀。

看法　不仅　告别　舍不得　专业　庆贺

1. 一年前我________家乡和亲友来到中国留学，现在中国已经成了我的第二个故乡。
2. 我在大学学习的________是经济学。
3. 学习语言________要记住一些语法、词语及其用法，还要多学习文化知识，了解这个国家的社会情况。
4. 我非常同意你的________，人不能只为自己活着。
5. 几乎所有的留学生都这样：刚来的时候不习惯，想家、想快点儿回国，可该走了，又________离开了。
6. 我希望三年后全班同学再来聚会，________你们获得学士学位。

（四）用“不仅”完成下列句子并大声朗读 Complete the following sentences with “不仅” and read them aloud

1. 大学生在学校________________，更要学会做人的道理。

2. 我来中国＿＿＿＿＿＿＿＿，还要＿＿＿＿＿＿＿＿。
3. 我们＿＿＿＿＿＿＿＿，更要提高读写的水平。
4. 爸爸希望你在校期间＿＿＿＿＿＿＿＿，还要锻炼意志。
5. 来这里半年多了，他＿＿＿＿＿＿＿＿，甚至连北京都没去过。
6. 这雪下了半天了，＿＿＿＿＿＿＿＿，还越下越大了。

（五）**完成下列会话并大声朗读** Complete the following conversations and read them aloud

1. A：我是黄春燕。老师，我想去看看您，不知道您现在方便不方便？
   B：＿＿＿＿＿＿＿＿＿＿＿＿＿＿＿＿＿＿＿＿。
2. A：你回国以后打算做什么？
   B：＿＿＿＿＿＿＿＿＿＿＿＿＿＿＿＿＿＿＿＿。
3. A：你什么时候产生这个想法的？
   B：＿＿＿＿＿＿＿＿＿＿＿＿＿＿＿＿＿＿＿＿。（早就）
4. A：你在大学是学什么专业的？
   B：＿＿＿＿＿＿＿＿＿＿＿＿＿＿＿＿＿＿＿＿。
5. A：＿＿＿＿＿＿＿＿＿＿＿＿＿＿＿＿＿＿＿＿？
   （有　什么体会　感觉　怎么样）
   B：这一年的经历使我终生难忘。这段时间，不仅提高了我的汉语水平，更重要的是，我还学会了许多书本上学不到的东西。不但增长了知识，也增长了见识，更增强了我学好汉语和独立生活的信心。
6. A：回去以后常联系吧，需要老师帮忙的，就发微信。只要能做到的，老师一定帮你。
   B：＿＿＿＿＿＿＿＿＿＿＿＿＿＿＿＿＿＿＿＿。（谢谢　保重）
7. A：大姐，你们都要走了，只有我和青木要留下来，不知道什么时候咱们能再见面呢？
   B：＿＿＿＿＿＿＿＿＿＿＿＿＿＿＿＿＿＿＿＿。（还会　见面）

8. A：好了，别哭了，我一定再回来。等你们俩把学士学位拿下来时，我们班同学一起来为你们庆贺，怎么样？

B：________________________。（好啊　一言为定）

（六）和同学一起表演课文 Act out the text with your classmates

（七）自由表达 Express yourself freely

和同学一起说说自己的留学生活。哪件事印象最深刻？什么人能让自己难以忘记？遇到过什么有趣的人或事？今后有什么打算？继续学习还是工作？留在中国还是回国？等等。

（八）读后说 Read the passage and say it

1. 朗读 Read aloud

一生难忘

——一个留学生的临别感言

不知不觉，一年就要过去了。刚来中国时，我连汉语都不会说，汉字也不认识，也没有朋友，感到非常难过，非常孤单。加上不习惯这里的气候，不习惯这里的饭菜，天天想家，还常以泪洗面。

感谢敬爱的老师们，给了我们父母般的关爱，亲切耐心地教我们学说汉语，学写汉字。

不到半年，我就习惯了。我学会了用汉语跟中国人交谈，这使我越来越喜欢这里的生活，越来越感谢父母送我来中国留学。

在即将告别母校，离别敬爱的老师，和同学们说再见的时候，我内心有的是不舍和留恋。

一年很短，但给我留下的美好回忆一生难忘。

美丽的校园里，到处都留下了我们的足迹：绿荫道上我们几乎天天来来往往，在草地上我们一起歌唱、聊天儿，课堂上常常带错儿的发言，换来的是满屋灿烂的笑脸。在体育馆里健身，在操场上跑圈儿、打球、打拳，周六我们一起骑车去爬山，一起在礼堂跳舞，一起在宿舍里交谈，一起逛大街，一起逛商店，一起去各种饭馆儿吃美味的中餐，一起去公园疯玩儿。

我们也一起去外地旅行，进行语言实践，还一起参加运动会，一起参加汉语节目表演。热闹的国际文化节，欢乐的同学生日宴，这一幕幕，一件件，一天天都不时地出现在我的眼前。

我们一起走过的路上，有欢笑也有眼泪，有孤独时想家的心酸，也有会说汉语带来的甘甜。

我结交了世界各国的朋友，尽管我们有不同的肤色、不同的文化，说着不同的语言，但共同的目的让我们心心相连。

最难忘的是我生病住院时，同学忙来忙去地为我办手续。老师来看我，给我送来她亲手做的热汤面。

在敬爱的老师们亲切耐心的教导和无微不至的关怀下，我们学说美丽的汉语，读写美丽的汉字，汉语像座桥，连通了我们的心田，使我们从陌生到熟悉，再到彼此成了好朋友而无话不谈。

感谢学校为我们提供了这个国际化的学习环境，在这里，我们不仅学习了汉语，学习了中国文化及相关的知识，我还从各国同学的身上了解了不同的文化与价值观，开阔了视野，有了国际化的胸怀和理念，懂得了开放和包容，明白了：美好的世界就应该——多元！

一年前我们在这里相逢，一年后我们将各奔前程，尽管不免伤感，但我知道，告别过去，是为了迎接更加美好的明天。

老师们的教导会激励着我们继续努力，不断向前。

衷心祝福敬爱的老师们身体健康、工作顺利、生活幸福美满。

衷心祝愿同学们在各自的岗位上成绩辉煌。

最后，我想说，老师们，同学们，我爱你们！

谢谢！再见！

小词典

难忘	nánwàng	动	cannot forget
临别	línbié	动	be at parting
感言	gǎnyán	名	words to express one's feelings or thoughts
即将	jíjiāng	副	be about to

心酸	xīn suān	形	feel sad
甘甜	gāntián	形	sweet
彼此	bǐcǐ	代	each other
提供	tígōng	动	provide
价值观	jiàzhíguān	名	sense of value
开阔	kāikuò	形、动	open; widen
视野	shìyě	名	view
胸怀	xiōnghuái	名、动	mind; have in mind
理念	lǐniàn	名	idea
包容	bāoróng	动	be tolerant
多元	duōyuán	形	diverse
不免	bùmiǎn	副	unavoidably
伤感	shānggǎn	形	sentimental; sad
激励	jīlì	动	encourage
不断	búduàn	副、动	continuously; constantly; continue
衷心	zhōngxīn	形	heartfelt
岗位	gǎngwèi	名	post; job
辉煌	huīhuáng	形	glorious

2. 回答下列问题 Answer the following questions

（1）刚来中国时，“我”是什么样的感受？

（2）“我”多长时间才习惯了留学生活？

（3）“我”最难忘的回忆是什么？

（4）这一年除了学汉语，“我”和同学们还做了什么？

（5）“我”这一年有哪些收获？

3. 你是 A，请你向 B 提问 Supposing you are A, ask B questions

（1）A: ______________________________？（刚　情况）

B：刚来中国时，我连汉语都不会说，汉字也不认识，也没有朋友，感到非常难过，非常孤单。加上不习惯这里的气候，不习惯这里的饭菜，天天想家，还会以泪洗面。

（2）A：____？

（多久　怎么样）

B：不到半年，我就习惯了。我学会了用汉语跟中国人交谈，这使我越来越喜欢这里的生活，越来越感谢父母送我来中国留学。

（3）A：____？（心情）

B：在即将告别母校，离别敬爱的老师，和同学们说再见的时候，我内心有的是不舍和留恋。

（4）A：____？（回忆）

B：美丽的校园里，到处都留下了我们的足迹：绿荫道上我们几乎天天来来往往，在草地上我们一起歌唱、聊天儿，课堂上常常带错儿的发言，换来的是满屋灿烂的笑脸。在体育馆里健身，在操场上跑圈儿、打球、打拳，周六我们一起骑车去爬山，一起在礼堂跳舞，一起在宿舍里交谈，一起逛大街，一起逛商店，一起去各种饭馆儿吃美味的中餐，一起去公园疯玩儿。我们也一起去外地旅行，进行语言实践，还一起参加运动会，一起参加汉语节目表演。热闹的国际文化节，欢乐的同学生日宴，这一幕幕，一件件，一天天都不时地出现在我的眼前。

（5）A：____？

（同学　关系）

B：我结交了世界各国的朋友，尽管我们有不同的肤色、不同的文化，说着不同的语言，但共同的目的让我们心心相连。

（6）A：____？（最）

B：最难忘的是我生病住院时，同学忙来忙去地为我办手续。老师来看我，给我送来她亲手做的热汤面。

（7）A：________________________？（收获）

B：在敬爱的老师们亲切耐心的教导和无微不至的关怀下，我们学说美丽的汉语，读写美丽的汉字，用汉语做桥梁，连通我们的心田，使我们从陌生到熟悉，再到彼此成了好朋友而无话不谈。

（8）A：________________________？（祝愿）

B：最后衷心祝福敬爱的老师们身体健康、工作顺利、生活幸福美满，祝愿同学们在各自的岗位上成绩辉煌。

4. 复述这篇课文 Retell this text

（九）朗读中国经典诗词，请注意语音语调 Read aloud the classic Chinese poem and pay attention to the pronunciation and intonation

Fúróng Lóu Sòng Xīn Jiàn
芙蓉 楼 送 辛 渐

[Táng] Wáng Chānglíng
[唐] 王 昌龄 （?—757）

Hán yǔ lián jiāng yè rù Wú, píngmíng sòng kè Chǔ Shān gū.
寒雨连 江 夜入吴，平明 送客楚 山 孤。

Luòyáng qīnyǒu rú xiāng wèn, yí piàn bīng xīn zài yù hú.
洛阳 亲友如相 问，一片 冰 心在玉壶。

（十）请欣赏下列著名的词句 Please enjoy the following famous saying

Shūshān yǒu lù qín wéi jìng, xuéhǎi wú yá kǔ zuò zhōu.
书山 有路 勤 为 径，学海 无涯苦作 舟。

Diligence is the way to knowledge,
and painstaking work is the boat to explore the endless sea of learning.

Dì-liùshísì kè Hòuhuì-yǒuqī

第六十四课 后会有期

Lesson 64 See you around

一 课文 Text

（马修是公司请来的工程师。现在他就要回国了，关经理举行宴会为他饯行）

关经理：时间过得真快，一转眼一年就过去了，马修就要回国了。今天我们在这儿聚会为他饯行。来，让我们举杯，祝马修身体健康、万事如意。干杯！

大　家：干杯！

马　修：这一年，承蒙各位关照，让我在中国工作和生活得十分愉快。马上要分别了，我真有点儿舍不得。

关经理：马修，一年来，你对我们公司的发展做出了很大的贡献。来，我代表总公司敬你一杯。

马　修：谢谢总经理。

关经理：真舍不得你离开呀，马修。你走以后，我们会想念你的。

马　修：我也会想念你们的。有机会的话，到法国来吧，我会陪你们好好逛逛巴黎，请你们品尝法国名菜。

关经理：我们一定有机会再见的，不是在巴黎，就是在北京。此情此景，让我想起了一句唐诗——海内存知己，天涯若比邻。不管我们在什么地方，离得多远，都像邻居一样，都是好朋友。你看，这句诗说的是不是我们现在的情景？

马　修：是呀，我们都是满世界飞的人。地球越来越小，今天分别，说不定什么时候就又见面了。

关经理：对！马修，什么时候还来？我们随时欢迎你再来。
马　修：我想明年，最迟后年。总之，咱们后会有期。
关经理：对，后会有期。来，让我们祝愿早日重逢，祝在座各位身体健康、工作顺利、平平安安、万事如意，干杯！
大　家：干杯！

二 生词 New Words

1	后会有期	hòuhuì-yǒuqī		see you around; meet again some day
2	举行	jǔxíng	动	hold (a meeting, banquet, etc.)
3	宴会	yànhuì	名	feast; banquet
4	饯行	jiànxíng	动	give a farewell dinner; see sb. off
5	转眼	zhuǎnyǎn	动	in an instant; in a flash
6	万事如意	wànshì-rúyì		realize all one's wishes
7	承蒙	chéngméng	动	be granted a favor
8	分别	fēnbié	动、副	part; say goodbye to each other; respectively
9	发展	fāzhǎn	动	develop
10	代表	dàibiǎo	动	represent; on behalf of
11	敬	jìng	动	toast
12	想念	xiǎngniàn	动	miss
13	品尝	pǐncháng	动	taste
14	名	míng		famous
15	此	cǐ	代	this
16	海内存知己，天涯若比邻	hǎinèi cún zhījǐ, tiānyá ruò bǐlín		long distance separates no bosom friends

17 邻居	línjū	名	neighbor
18 迟	chí	形	late
19 祝愿	zhùyuàn	动	wish
20 早日	zǎorì	副、名	soon; at an early date
21 重逢	chóngféng	动	meet again
22 在座	zàizuò	动	be present (at a meeting, banquet, etc.)

专名 Zhuānmíng Proper Nouns

1 巴黎	Bālí	Paris
2 唐诗	Táng Shī	poetry of the Tang Dynasty

三 注释 Notes

(一) 不是……就是……

"不是……就是……"表示在两个事物或情况中肯定有一个是所需要的、所要选择的。例如：

"不是……就是……" means that one of two things or situations must be needed or chosen. For example:

1. 我们一定有机会再见的，不是在巴黎，就是在北京。
2. 我一定会再来的，不是明年就是后年。
3. 他每次都考得很好，不是一百分就是九十多。

(二) 总之

"总之"也说"总而言之"，用来总括前面所说的。例如：

"总之" can also be said as "总而言之". It is used to summarize what was said before. For example:

1. 学汉语听说很重要，读写也同样重要，总之，听说读写都很重要。
2. 我们家乡夏天不热，冬天也不冷，总之，一年四季都很舒服。

3. 学习外语不能只用耳朵听，还要用眼看、开口说、动手写。总之，眼、耳、口、手、脑，都要动起来。

（三）早日

“早日”表示早早儿地、时间提前地，在句中做状语。例如：

“早日” means “as soon as possible” or “well in advance”. It is used as an adverbial in a sentence. For example:

1. 我希望能早日拿到 HSK 中级证书。
2. 祝你早日出院。
3. 爸爸妈妈盼望（pànwàng, look forward to）我早日学成回国。

四 练习 Exercises

（一）朗读 Read aloud

1. 朗读下列发音相近的词语 Read aloud the following words with similar pronunciation

jǔ bēi 举杯	jùbèi 具备	jìng jiù 敬酒	jīngjiǔ 经久
qíngjǐng 情景	qīngjìng 清净	zǎorì 早日	zhāorì 朝日
zǒngzhī 总之	zōngzhǐ 宗旨	xiǎngniàn 想念	xiāngjiàn 相见

2. 朗读下列短语和句子 Read the following phrases and sentences aloud

饯行：为你饯行　为朋友饯行　给同学饯行　给同事饯行

承蒙：承蒙关照　承蒙照顾　承蒙厚爱　承蒙指导　承蒙教导

想念：想念父母　想念亲人　想念弟弟　想念姐姐　想念妹妹

逛：逛巴黎　逛商店　逛书店　逛书市　逛公园　逛超市　逛大街

名：名菜　名酒　名茶　名人　名曲　名画　名著

随时：随时准备着　随时跟我联系　随时等我的消息

祝愿：祝愿我们早日重逢　祝愿你早日找到理想的工作

祝愿你万事如意

（二）**替换并朗读** Replace and read aloud

1. 来，让我们举杯，祝马修一路平安，干杯！

祝吉米生日快乐
祝小玉早日拿到学士学位
为你找到了好工作
为在座的朋友们身体健康
祝我们双方合作愉快
为我们两国人民的友谊

2. 这一年，承蒙各位关照，让我在中国生活得十分愉快。

各位领导关照　老师的关爱
朋友们的帮助　总经理的关心

3. 你对我们公司的发展做出了很大的贡献。

她	中医的发展
他	公司的科研
马校长	教育事业
这些志愿者	环保事业
这位先生	发展我们两国的友好关系

4. 我们随时欢迎你再来。

回来　回国　加入　参加

（三）**选词填空并朗读下列句子** Choose the appropriate words to fill in the blanks and read aloud the following sentences

转眼　说不定　十分　饯行　贡献　后会有期　就是　的话

1. 马修是公司请来的工程师。现在他就要回国了，关经理举行宴会为他________。
2. 时间过得真快，一________一年就过去了，马修就要回国了。今天我们在这儿聚会为他饯行。来，让我们举杯，祝马修身体健康、万事如意。干杯！
3. 这一年，承蒙各位关照，让我在中国工作和生活得________愉快。马上要分别了，我真有点儿舍不得。
4. 马修，一年来，你对我们公司的发展做出了很大的________。来，我代表总公司敬你一杯。
5. 我也会想念你们的。有机会________，到法国来吧，我会陪你们好好逛逛巴黎，请你们品尝法国名菜。
6. 我们一定有机会再见的，不是在巴黎，________在北京。
7. 是呀，我们都是满世界飞的人。地球越来越小，今天分别，________什么时候就又见面了。
8. A：马修，什么时候还来？我们随时欢迎你再来。
   B：我想明年，最迟后年。总之，咱们________。

承蒙　万事如意　恋恋不舍　为　祝愿　举杯

1. 来自美国的白修德教授就要回国了，今天校长举行宴会，________他饯行。
2. 让我们________，为在座朋友们的健康、为我们的友谊，干杯！
3. 我来中国以后，________校长和各位的关照，生活工作得十分愉快。
4. 我刚来中国时很不习惯，现在就要回国了，却感到________，不愿离开。

5. ________你早日梦想成真。
6. 祝在座各位生活幸福、身体健康、________。

（四）完成下列句子并大声朗读 Complete the following sentences and read them aloud

1. 听说你住院了，祝你________________。（早日）
2. 希望你来留学的手续办得顺利，________________。（早日）
3. 爸爸妈妈希望我好好学习，________________。（早日）
4. 加我的微信吧，我们________________。（随时）
5. 来中国以后，我________________，要好好学习汉语和中国文化。（随时 提醒）
6. 我们班十几个同学，有的来自亚洲，有的来自欧洲，还有的来自非洲和美洲，________________。（总之）
7. 学校教育不仅要重视智育，更要重视德育，同时，还要加强体育和美育，________________，这样才能为社会培养出需要的人才。（总之）
8. 学习汉语，听说很重要，读写也同样重要，________________。（总之）

（五）完成下列会话并大声朗读 Complete the following conversations and read them aloud

1. A：今天我们在这儿聚会，________________________，干杯！
   B：干杯！
2. A：马修，你在这儿过得怎么样？
   B：________________________________。（承蒙 关照 愉快）
3. A：一年来，你对我们公司的发展做出了很大的贡献。来，我代表总公司敬您一杯。
   B：________________________________。（谢谢）
4. A：你走以后，我们会想念你的。
   B：________________________________。
   （也 有机会 来 逛逛 巴黎 品尝）

5. A："海内存知己，天涯若比邻"，你看，这句诗说的是不是我们现在的情景？

B：________________________________。

（满世界　地球　越来越）

6. A：你什么时候还来？我们随时欢迎你再来。

B：________________________________。

（明年　后年　总之　后会有期）

（六）和同学一起表演课文 Act out the text with your classmates

（七）自由表达 Express yourself freely

和同学一起举行一个告别宴会，每个人准备两三分钟的告别词，你会跟大家说什么？

（八）读后说 Read the passage and say it

1. 朗读 Read aloud

换一个角度

两年前，我在一家大型企业工作。有一次，单位请了一位大学教授给全体管理人员讲授"企业可持续发展战略"。快结束时，教授给我们出了一道有趣的思考题：在很远的地方发现了一座金矿。为了得到黄金，人们蜂拥而至，可一条大江挡住了必经之路。如果是你们，会怎么办？

教授刚说完考题，会场就热闹了起来，有人说游过去，有人说绕道过去。但教授却笑而不语。过了一会儿，教授才说，为什么非要去淘金？为什么不可以买一条船搞运输，接送那些淘金的人？这样照样可以发财致富！人们为了发财，即使票价再贵，也心甘情愿买票上船。因为前面是金矿啊！

我们茅塞顿开。

对于生活中的许多问题，当我们无所适从时，为什么不能换一个角度去思考呢？是的，在智者眼里，困境往往意味着一个潜在的机遇。

小词典

角度	jiǎodù	名	point of view; angle
大型	dàxíng	形	large; large-scale
企业	qǐyè	名	enterprise
讲授	jiǎngshòu	动	lecture; teach
持续	chíxù	动	continue; last
战略	zhànlüè	名	strategy
金矿	jīnkuàng	名	gold mine
蜂拥而至	fēngyōng'érzhì		swarm
挡	dǎng	动	keep off; ward off
必经之路	bìjīngzhīlù		only way
绕道	rào dào	动	make a detour
淘金	táo jīn	动	wash (for gold)
运输	yùnshū	动	transport
发财	fā cái	动	become rich; make a fortune
致富	zhìfù	动	become rich; make a fortune
心甘情愿	xīngān-qíngyuàn		willingly
茅塞顿开	máosè-dùnkāi		be suddenly enlightened
无所适从	wúsuǒshìcóng		at a loose end; not know what to do
智者	zhìzhě	名	wise man
困境	kùnjìng	名	dilemma
意味着	yìwèizhe	动	signify; mean
潜在	qiánzài	形	potential; hidden
机遇	jīyù	名	opportunity; chance

2. 回答下列问题 Answer the following questions

（1）两年前“我”在什么单位工作?

（2）单位请教授讲什么?

（3）教授给大家出了一道什么思考题?

（4）大家都是怎么思考的?

（5）教授要大家怎么思考?

（6）“我”从教授的话里得到了什么启示?

3. 你是 A，请你向 B 提问 Supposing you are A, ask B questions

（1）A: ________________________?（哪儿）

B: 两年前，我在一家大型企业工作。

（2）A: ________________________?（什么）

B: 单位请了一位大学教授给全体管理人员讲授“企业的可持续发展战略”。

（3）A: ________________________?（什么　思考题）

B: 快结束时，教授给我们出了一道有趣的思考题：在很远的地方发现了一座金矿。为了得到黄金，人们蜂拥而至，可一条大江挡住了必经之路。如果是你们，会怎么办?

（4）A: ________________________?（怎么）

B: 有人说游过去，有人说绕道走。

（5）A: ________________________?（怎么）

B: 过了一会儿，教授才说，为什么非要去淘金? 为什么不可以买一条船搞运输，接送那些淘金的人? 这样照样可以发财致富!

（6）A: ________________________?（为什么）

B: 因为在教授看来，人们为了发财，即使票价再贵，也心甘情愿买票上船。

（7）A: ________________________?（什么　启发）

B: 对于生活中的许多问题，当我们无所适从时，为什么不能换一个角度去思考? 在智者眼里，困境往往意味着一个潜在的机遇。

4. 复述这篇课文 Retell this text

（九）**朗读中国经典诗词，请注意语音语调** Read aloud the classic Chinese poem and pay attention to the pronunciation and intonation

Song Dù Shàofǔ Zhī Rèn Shǔ Zhōu
送杜少府之任蜀州

[Táng] Wáng Bó
［唐］王 勃（650—676）

Chéngquè fǔ sān Qín，fēngyān wàng wǔ jīn.
城阙辅三秦，风烟望五津。

Yǔ jūn líbié yì，tóng shì huànyóurén.
与君离别意，同是宦游人。

Hǎinèi cún zhījǐ，tiānyá ruò bǐlín.
海内存知己，天涯若比邻。

Wúwéi zài qílù，érnǚ gòng zhān jīn.
无为在歧路，儿女共沾巾。

（十）**请欣赏下列著名的词句** Please enjoy the following famous saying

Cháng Jiāng hòu làng tuī qián làng，shì shàng xīn rén huàn jiù rén.
长江后浪推前浪，世上新人换旧人。

As in the Yangtze River waves urge waves,
so the younger generation excels the older generation.

词汇表 Vocabulary

A

哎	āi	叹	*expressing surprise or dissatisfaction*	50
爱好	àihào	动、名	be fond of; hobby	57
安排	ānpái	动	arrange; plan	52
岸	àn	名	bank; shore	61
暗暗	àn’àn	副	secretly; inwardly; to oneself	56

B

拜师	bài shī	动	take sb. as a one’s teacher	57
绊	bàn	动	(cause to) stumble	49
包容	bāoróng	动	be tolerant	63
保护	bǎohù	动	protect	52
保重	bǎozhòng	动	take care of	63
报道	bàodào	动、名	report	57
报名	bào míng	动	apply; sign up	49
碑林	bēilín	名	forest of steles	62
悲壮	bēizhuàng	形	solemn and stirring	57
本科	běnkē	名	regular college course; undergraduate course	63
本来	běnlái	副、形	originally; original	49
本领	běnlǐng	名	skill; ability	57
彼此	bǐcǐ	代	each other	63
必经之路	bìjīngzhīlù		only way	64
闭	bì	动	close; shut	55
边	biān	名	edge; margin	54
遍	biàn	动	all over; everywhere	52

遍布	biànbù	动	be found everywhere; spread all over	50
标准	biāozhǔn	名、形	standard; standardized	54
冰川	bīngchuān	名	glacier	58
冰灯	bīngdēng	名	ice lantern	62
冰雕	bīngdiāo	名	ice sculpture	62
兵马俑	bīngmǎyǒng	名	terracotta warriors and horses	62
病房	bìngfáng	名	ward (of a hospital)	59
病人	bìngrén	名	patient	60
病逝	bìngshì	动	die of an illness	55
玻璃	bōli	名	glass	62
脖子	bózi	名	neck	50
不断	búduàn	副、动	continuously; constantly; continue	63
捕杀	bǔshā	动	catch and kill (an animal)	58
不得不	bùdébù		cannot but; have to	56
不仅	bùjǐn	连	not only; beyond a quantity or scope	63
不久	bùjiǔ	形	soon; before long	50
不可思议	bùkě-sīyì		inconceivable; unimaginable	50
不免	bùmiǎn	副	unavoidably	63
不然	bùrán	连、形	or else; if not; otherwise	59
不由得	bùyóude	动、副	cannot help	51
布	bù	名	cloth	53
C 擦	cā	动	wipe	53
材料	cáiliào	名	material	52
财务	cáiwù	名	finance	62
裁判	cáipàn	名、动	referee; judge	49
采摘	cǎizhāi	动	pick; pluck	61
参赛	cānsài	动	take part in a match	49
参与	cānyù	动	participate in; take part in	49
惨	cǎn	形	serious; calamitous	51

草原	cǎoyuán	名	grassland	58
曾经	céngjīng	副	once; ever	55
插	chā	动	insert	53
车轮	chēlún	名	wheel	58
沉	chén	动、形	sink; heavy	51
沉思	chénsī	动	ruminate; contemplate	52
称	chēng	动	weigh	51
称赞	chēngzàn	动	praise	51
成功	chénggōng	动、形	succeed; successful	54
承蒙	chéngméng	动	be granted a favor	64
秤	chèng	名	balance; steelyard	51
吃	chī	动	suffer; incur; bear	51
吃惊	chī jīng	动	surprise	49
迟	chí	形	late	64
持续	chíxù	动	continue; last	64
充分	chōngfèn	形	full	61
重逢	chóngféng	动	meet again	64
出色	chūsè	形	excellent; extremely good	57
出书	chū shū		have (a book) published	57
出院	chū yuàn	动	be discharged from hospital	59
初步	chūbù	形	preliminary; initial	63
厨师	chúshī	名	cook	52
船票	chuánpiào	名	steamer ticket; boat or ship ticket	61
创作	chuàngzuò	动、名	compose; composition	55
吹	chuī	动	blow; puff	53
春卷儿	chūnjuǎnr	名	spring roll (a thin sheet of dough, rolled, stuffed, and fried)	63
此	cǐ	代	this	64
刺激	cìjī	动	stimulate	50

从而	cóng'ér	连	thus; thereby; hence	50
醋	cù	名	vinegar	54
催	cuī	动	urge; hurry	61
搓	cuō	动	rub with the hands	54
D 答应	dāying	动	agree	50
达到	dá dào	动	achieve; attain; reach	50
打点滴	dǎ diǎndī		have an intravenous drip	60
打盹儿	dǎ dǔnr	动	doze off; take (or have) a nap	57
打滑	dǎhuá	动	slip	58
打火机	dǎhuǒjī	名	lighter	53
打算	dǎsuàn	动、名	intend; plan; intention	61
大臣	dàchén	名	minister	51
大胆	dàdǎn	形	bold; brave	54
大师	dàshī	名	master	61
大型	dàxíng	形	large; large-scale	64
（大）象	(dà) xiàng	名	elephant	51
大意	dàyi	形	careless	51
待	dāi	动	stay	60
代表	dàibiǎo	动	represent; on behalf of	64
代替	dàitì	动	take the place of	59
带领	dàilǐng	动	lead; guide	58
当时	dāngshí	名	at that time	51
挡	dǎng	动	keep off; ward off	64
刀口	dāokǒu	名	cut; incision	60
导游	dǎoyóu	动、名	guide; tour guide service; tour guide	62
岛	dǎo	名	island	55
倒	dǎo	动	fall; tumble down	49
倒	dào	副	*contrary to what is expected or thought*	52
道理	dàolǐ	名	truth; principle; reason	61

	得奖	dé jiǎng		win a prize	55
	滴水之恩，当涌泉相报	dī shuǐ zhī ēn, dāng yǒng quán xiāng bào		Receive drips of water when in need, and return the kindness with a spring.	61
	底	dǐ	名	bottom	54
	地板	dìbǎn	名	floor	53
	地球	dìqiú	名	earth	58
	地质	dìzhì	名	geology	58
	点	diǎn	动	light (a fire)	53
	点球	diǎnqiú	名	penalty kick	51
	垫	diàn	动	pad	58
	叼	diāo	动	hold in the mouth	58
	掉	diào	动	shed; fall	63
	懂事	dǒng shì	形	sensible	55
	动员	dòngyuán	动	mobilize	58
	独立	dúlì	动	do sth. on one's own	63
	段	duàn	量	section; part; paragraph	54
	队员	duìyuán	名	team member	51
	墩布	dūnbù	名	mop; swab	53
	顿	dùn	量	*a measure word used to indicate frequency*	54
	多元	duōyuán	形	diverse	63
	夺冠	duó guàn	动	win the championship	49
E	摁	èn	动	press	54
F	发表	fābiǎo	动	publish (articles, paintings, songs, etc. in a periodical)	57
	发财	fā cái	动	become rich; make a fortune	64
	发动	fādòng	动	start up	58
	发烧	fā shāo	动	have a fever	59
	发现	fāxiàn	动	discover; find	52

发展	fāzhǎn	动	develop	64
发作	fāzuò	动	(of latent things) act up; suddenly break out or show effect	59
罚	fá	动	punish	51
翻译	fānyì	动	translate	55
反问	fǎnwèn	动	ask (a question) in reply	49
反正	fǎnzhèng	副	*used to indicate the same result despite different circumstances*	54
放飞	fàngfēi	动	set free; free	62
放假	fàng jià	动	take a holiday	61
飞	fēi	动	fly	62
分别	fēnbié	动、副	part; say goodbye to each other; respectively	64
吩咐	fēnfù	动	order; tell	51
纷纷	fēnfēn	副	one after another	51
份	fèn	量	*a measure word for newspapers or magazines*	52
丰富多彩	fēngfù-duōcǎi		rich and varied	53
风光	fēngguāng	名	landscape	62
风能	fēngnéng	名	wind energy	58
风俗	fēngsú	名	custom	56
疯	fēng	动、形	play crazily; crazy	57
蜂拥而至	fēngyōng'érzhì		swarm	64
抚摸	fǔmō	动	caress; stroke	62
辅导	fǔdǎo	动	tutor; give guidance in study or training	50
负责	fùzé	动、形	be responsible for; be in charge of; responsible	49
复杂	fùzá	形	complicated; complex	50

G

盖	gài	动	put a cover (over...); cover	54
盖儿	gàir	名	lid; cover	54
甘甜	gāntián	形	sweet	63

杆	gǎn	量	*a measure word for implements with a shaft*	51
赶	gǎn	动	hurry	59
赶快	gǎnkuài	副	at once; quickly	59
敢	gǎn	动	dare	54
感情	gǎnqíng	名	friendly contacts	53
感染	gǎnrǎn	动	infect	60
感言	gǎnyán	名	words to express one's feelings or thoughts	63
擀	gǎn	动	roll (dough, etc. with a rolling pin)	54
岗位	gǎngwèi	名	post; job	63
高尔夫球	gāo'ěrfūqiú	名	golf	56
高级	gāojí	形	high-grade; high-level	56
高亢	gāokàng	形	(of voice) loud and sonorous	57
高尚	gāoshàng	形	noble	49
告别	gào bié	动	say goodbye	63
告辞	gàocí	动	bid farewell; say goodbye (to sb.)	63
歌唱	gēchàng	动	sing	57
歌唱家	gēchàngjiā	名	singer	57
歌剧	gējù	名	opera	55
各	gè	代、副	each; apiece	49
各就各位	gèjiù-gèwèi		on your marks	49
跟随	gēnsuí	动	follow	51
公布	gōngbù	动	make public	56
公费	gōngfèi	名	funded by the state or the collective	56
公开	gōngkāi	形、动	public; make public	57
拱	gǒng	动	(of an animal) dig with the snout	58
共同	gòngtóng	形	common	58
贡献	gòngxiàn	动、名	contribute; contribution	55
估计	gūjì	动	estimate; appraise; reckon	60

股	gǔ	量	*a measure word for gas, smell or strength*	56
固定	gùdìng	动、形	fix; fixed	61
故意	gùyì	副	on purpose; consciously	51
怪	guài	形、副	strange; odd; strangely; oddly	55
关于	guānyú	介	about; with regard to	55
观赏	guānshǎng	动	enjoy the sight of	61
馆子	guǎnzi	名	restaurant; eatery	52
管	guǎn	动	be in charge of	62
归	guī	动	return; go or come back	62
棍儿	gùnr	名	stick; rod	54
锅	guō	名	pot	54
国籍	guójí	名	nationality	53
果然	guǒrán	副	sure enough; really; as expected	52

H

海内存知己，天涯若比邻	hǎinèi cún zhījǐ, tiānyá ruò bǐlín		long distance separates no bosom friends	64
害怕	hài pà	动	fear; afraid	62
喊	hǎn	动	call; yell; shout	49
毫不犹豫	háo bù yóuyù		without the least hesitation	56
好样儿的	hǎoyàngrde	名	great fellow	49
呵护	hēhù	动	take good care of	62
和蔼	hé'ǎi	形	nice; kind	60
红牌儿	hóngpáir	名	red card	51
后悔	hòuhuǐ	动	regret; repent	50
后会有期	hòuhuì-yǒuqī		see you around; meet again some day	64
蝴蝶	húdié	名	butterfly	62
虎	hǔ	名	tiger	51
互	hù	副	mutually	52
花瓶	huāpíng	名	vase	53

滑	huá	动、形	slip; slippery	56
滑冰	huá bīng	动	skate	56
滑雪	huá xuě	动	ski	56
环保	huánbǎo	名、形	environmental protection; eco-friendly	52
环境	huánjìng	名	environment	52
恍然大悟	huǎngrán-dàwù		realize all of a sudden	61
辉煌	huīhuáng	形	glorious	63
婚礼	hūnlǐ	名	wedding	61
混合	hùnhé	动	mix; mingle	52
和	huó	动	mix (flour) with water	54
火车票	huǒchēpiào	名	railway ticket	61
火候	huǒhou	名	level of accomplishment or sophistication	51
祸福与共	huòfú-yǔgòng		go through thick and thin together	58

J

几乎	jīhū	副	nearly; almost	52
叽里咕噜	jīligūlū	拟声	talk indistinctly or inaudibly about	49
机票	jīpiào	名	air ticket	61
机遇	jīyù	名	opportunity; chance	64
激励	jīlì	动	encourage	63
及时	jíshí	形	timely	59
吉他	jítā	名	guitar	53
即将	jíjiāng	副	be about to	63
急救	jíjiù	动	(give) first-aid to sb.	59
急救车	jíjiùchē	名	ambulance	59
急忙	jímáng	副	hastily; hurriedly; in a hurry	52
急性	jíxìng	形	acute	59
疾病	jíbìng	名	disease; illness	50
计划	jìhuà	动、名	plan	61
记号	jìhao	名	mark; sign	51

纪念	jìniàn	动、名	commemorate; commemoration	62
纪念品	jìniànpǐn	名	souvenir	62
加劲儿	jiā jìnr	动	put more energy into	53
加油	jiā yóu	动	come on	49
家伙	jiāhuo	名	guy	51
家属	jiāshǔ	名	family member	59
家乡	jiāxiāng	名	hometown	57
家园	jiāyuán	名	home; homeland	58
假期	jiàqī	名	vacation; holiday	61
价值观	jiàzhíguān	名	sense of value	63
见面	jiàn miàn	动	meet; see	63
饯行	jiànxíng	动	give a farewell dinner; see sb. off	64
讲授	jiǎngshòu	动	lecture; teach	64
奖学金	jiǎngxuéjīn	名	scholarship	56
交流	jiāoliú	动	interchange; exchange	53
交响乐	jiāoxiǎngyuè	名	symphony	55
郊外	jiāowài	名	outskirt	57
角度	jiǎodù	名	point of view; angle	64
搅	jiǎo	动	stir	54
教导	jiàodǎo	动	teach	62
教练	jiàoliàn	名	coach	51
教师	jiàoshī	名	teacher	63
教学相长	jiàoxué- -xiāngzhǎng		mutual advance between teaching and studying	63
教育	jiàoyù	动、名	educate; education	63
杰出	jiéchū	形	outstanding	55
结伴儿	jié bànr	动	go with	62
结识	jiéshí	动	get acquainted with sb.; get to know sb.	52
解释	jiěshì	动	explain	49

解说	jiěshuō	动	explain orally	52
解说词	jiěshuōcí	名	(written) caption; (oral) commentary	52
金矿	jīnkuàng	名	gold mine	64
尽管	jǐnguǎn	副、连	though; although	52
尽快	jǐnkuài	副	as quickly (soon or early) as possible	50
进修	jìnxiū	动	(often on leave from one's position for a set time) engage in advanced studies	50
劲头儿	jìntóur	名	vigor; spirit	56
禁区	jìnqū	名	penalty area (in certain types of ball games)	51
经过	jīngguò	动、名	after; through	59
经络	jīngluò	名	main and collateral channel	50
经验	jīngyàn	名	experience	52
惊呆	jīngdāi		stupefied; stunned	58
惊险	jīngxiǎn	形	breathtaking; thrilling	58
惊讶	jīngyà	形	surprised; astonished	57
精神	jīngshén	名	spirit	49
精心	jīngxīn	形	careful; meticulous	61
景观	jǐngguān	名	landscape	62
敬	jìng	动	toast	64
敬慕	jìngmù	动	worship	55
举行	jǔxíng	动	hold (a meeting, banquet, etc.)	64
举世闻名	jǔshì-wénmíng		world-famous	56
巨大	jùdà	形	enormous; tremendous	55
句型	jùxíng	名	sentence pattern	54
剧院	jùyuàn	名	theater	50
决定	juédìng	动、名	decide; decision	61
决赛	juésài	动	play in the final	55
觉醒	juéxǐng	动	awaken	58
绝望	jué wàng	动	despair	58

均	jūn	副	all; without exception	56
K 开	kāi	动	boil	54
开发	kāifā	动	develop; exploit	58
开阔	kāikuò	形、动	open; widen	63
开心	kāixīn	形、动	happy; feel happy	49
砍伐	kǎnfá	动	fell (a tree)	58
可见	kějiàn	连	it shows; that proves	58
可怕	kěpà	形	horrible; dreadful; terrible	58
可惜	kěxī	形	regrettable	56
刻苦	kèkǔ	形	assiduous; hard-working	57
客座	kèzuò	形	visiting	55
课间	kèjiān	名	break (between classes)	52
坑	kēng	动、名	defraud; pit; hole	58
扣除	kòuchú	动	deduct	62
跨	kuà	动	stride; stride leap	49
宽裕	kuānyù	形	well-to-do	61
况且	kuàngqiě	连	besides	61
困境	kùnjìng	名	dilemma	64
L 蜡烛	làzhú	名	candle	53
栏（杆）	lán (gān)	名	hurdle	49
阑尾炎	lánwěiyán	名	appendicitis	59
蓝天	lán tiān		blue sky	58
狼	láng	名	wolf	58
捞	lāo	动	scoop up (from liquid)	54
老	lǎo	副	always; all the time	60
老是	lǎoshì	副	always; all the time	51
老鼠	lǎoshǔ	名	mouse	54
落枕	lào zhěn	动	have a stiff neck (caused by cold or awkward sleeping posture)	50

泪	lèi	名	tear; teardrop	49
礼物	lǐwù	名	gift; present	52
理解	lǐjiě	动	comprehend; understand	55
理念	lǐniàn	名	idea	63
历史	lìshǐ	名	history	55
立志	lì zhì	动	be determined	57
利用	lìyòng	动	make use of	61
连忙	liánmáng	副	at once	59
连载	liánzǎi	动	serialize	55
联络	liánluò	动	contact	53
量	liáng	动	measure	59
亮	liàng	形、动	shining; dawn	57
料理	liàolǐ	名、动	food and drink; cuisine; cook	52
邻居	línjū	名	neighbor	64
临别	línbié	动	be at parting	63
临门	línmén	动	face the goal	51
临门一脚	línmén yì jiǎo		go for the goal	51
领先	lǐng xiān	动	lead; be in the lead	51
另	lìng	代、副	another; in addition	57
流	liú	动	shed (tears)	49
流泪	liúlèi	动	shed tears	49
路过	lùguò	动	pass by or through (a place)	60
路线	lùxiàn	名	itinerary	61
旅伴	lǚbàn	名	traveling companion; fellow traveler	61
旅馆	lǚguǎn	名	hotel	61
旅行团	lǚxíngtuán	名	tour group	61
旅游	lǚyóu	动	tour	61
M 马马虎虎	mǎmǎhūhū	形	not very good; so-so; not so bad	56
盲目	mángmù	形	blind; aimless	57

茅塞顿开	máosè-dùnkāi		be suddenly enlightened	64
美不胜收	měibú-shèngshōu		there are more beautiful things than the eyes can take in	62
美妙	měimiào	形	wonderful; beautiful; splendid	55
美食家	měishíjiā	名	gourmet	52
美中不足	měizhōng-bùzú		fly in the ointment	56
门	mén	量	*a measure word for fields of study or technical training*	56
迷人	mírén	形	enchanting; charming	62
秘书长	mìshūzhǎng	名	secretary-general	58
面粉	miànfěn	名	flour	54
面皮儿	miànpír	名	wrapper (of dumplings, etc.)	54
灭	miè	动	(of a light, fire, etc.) go out	53
民歌	míngē	名	folk song	57
名	míng		famous	64
名贵	míngguì	形	rare; precious	61
名片	míngpiàn	名	name card	60
名气	míngqi	名	reputation; fame	57
明智	míngzhì	形	sensible; wise	56
命运	mìngyùn	名	destiny	58
陌生	mòshēng	形	strange; unfamiliar	60
木偶	mù'ǒu	名	puppet	49
N 难忘	nánwàng	动	cannot forget	63
能源	néngyuán	名	energy	58
念	niàn	动	read	50
念念不忘	niànniàn-búwàng		constantly bear in mind; always keep in mind	56
捏	niē	动	squeeze	54
浓厚	nónghòu	形	strong; deep	55

O	偶尔	ǒu'ěr	副	now and then; sometimes	56
P	趴	pā	动	bend over; lean on	57
	啪	pā	拟声	*indicating the sound of clapping, striking, or shooting*	49
	拍子	pāizi	名	(of music) rhythm	57
	派	pài	动	send; dispatch	59
	盘子	pánzi	名	plate	54
	泡	pào	动、名	make (tea); bubble	63
	陪	péi	动	keep company; accompany	59
	赔	péi	动	compensate for	62
	配合	pèihé	动	coordinate; cooperate	51
	皮儿	pír	名	(dumpling) wrapper	54
	片儿汤	piànrtāng	名	flat pieces of dough served with soup	54
	漂	piāo	动	float	54
	票	piào	名	ticket	61
	品尝	pǐncháng	动	taste	64
	平时	píngshí	名	ordinary times; normal times	52
	平实	píngshí	形	plain; simple and unadorned	55
	破坏	pòhuài	动	destroy	58
	扑	pū	动	(of a soccer game) save (a goal)	51
	铺	pū	动	spread	53
Q	其实	qíshí	副	in fact; as a matter of fact; actually	50
	其他	qítā	代	other	55
	奇	qí		strange	62
	奇怪	qíguài	形	strange	49
	奇迹	qíjì	名	miracle	61
	企业	qǐyè	名	enterprise	64
	气氛	qìfēn	名	atmosphere	53
	气球	qìqiú	名	balloon	52

气色	qìsè	名	complexion	60
器官	qìguān	名	organ	50
千变万化	qiānbiàn--wànhuà		ever-changing	62
牵	qiān	动	lead along	51
谦和	qiānhé	形	modest and gentle	55
签字	qiān zì	动	sign; write one's signature	59
前锋	qiánfēng	名	(in basketball, soccer, etc.) forward; player whose task is to attack or score	51
前途	qiántú	名	future; prospect	56
潜在	qiánzài	形	potential; hidden	64
欠	qiàn	动	not enough	51
枪	qiāng	名	gun	58
强	qiáng	形	strong; powerful	51
桥梁	qiáoliáng	名	bridge	56
切	qiē	动	cut	51
切除	qiēchú	动	remove; cut off	59
亲	qīn	形	related by blood or marriage	50
去世	qùshì	动	die; pass away	55
全国	quánguó	名	whole nation (or country)	56
全身	quánshēn	名	all over (the body); from head to foot	50
却	què	副	but; yet; however	57
群	qún	量	pack; throng	58
R 绕道	rào dào	动	make a detour	64
热爱	rè'ài	动	love	57
热烈	rèliè	形	lively; warm	53
人类	rénlèi	名	mankind; human	58
认	rèn	动	learn to read; recognize	63
认为	rènwéi	动	think; believe	50

圣贤	shèngxián	名	sage; saint	55
胜局	shèngjú	名	victory; success	51
失约	shī yuē	动	fail to keep an appointment; break one's promise	60
师范	shīfàn	名	normal school	63
诗	shī	名	poetry; poem	62
诗歌	shīgē	名	poetry	57
施主	shīzhǔ	名	(monks' or priests' form of address for) those who give money or food to the monastery or Taoist temple	61
十分	shífēn	副	very	51
石头	shítou	名	stone	51
实力	shílì	名	actual strength; power	51
实现	shíxiàn	动	realize; come true	53
视野	shìyě	名	view	63
收音机	shōuyīnjī	名	radio	55
手术	shǒushù	名	operation; surgery	59
手腕儿	shǒuwànr	名	wrist	56
手续	shǒuxù	名	procedure	49
守门员	shǒuményuán	名	goalkeeper	51
寿星	shòuxing	名	the one whose birthday is being celebrated	53
受伤	shòu shāng	动	be injured; be wounded	49
疏通	shūtōng	动	dredge	50
输	shū	动	lose (in a game)	51
熟	shú	形	make well-cooked	54
属	shǔ	动	be born in the year of	53
属于	shǔyú	动	belong to	53
束	shù	量	bundle; bunch	60
树枝	shùzhī	名	twig; branch	58
说不定	shuōbudìng	副	perhaps; maybe	59

四周	sìzhōu	名	all around; on all sides	53
松	sōng	名	pine (tree)	62
送行	sòng xíng	动	see sb. off	57
肃然起敬	sùrán-qǐjìng		be filled with deep veneration	49
蒜	suàn	名	garlic	54
算	suàn	动	consider; regard as; count as	57
随着	suízhe	介	(along) with	56
锁定	suǒdìng	动	(of a game) be in the bag	51

T

抬	tái	动	lift; raise	50
太阳能	tàiyángnéng	名	solar energy	58
谈不上	tánbushàng		far from; be out of the question	55
汤	tāng	名	soup	54
汤面	tāngmiàn	名	noodles in soup	60
淘金	táo jīn	动	wash (for gold)	64
提高	tí gāo	动	raise; improve	51
提供	tígōng	动	provide	63
体温	tǐwēn	名	(body) temperature	59
体育	tǐyù	名	sports	49
挑选	tiāoxuǎn	动	select	61
条件	tiáojiàn	名	condition	60
铁路	tiělù	名	railway	61
通知	tōngzhī	动、名	inform; notice	59
同行	tóngháng	名	peer; counterpart	63
同时	tóngshí	连、名	at the same time; contemporary	52
童话	tónghuà	名	fairy tale	62
痛心	tòngxīn	形	distressed; pained; grieved	58
头狼	tóuláng	名	alpha wolf; leader wolf	58
头重脚轻	tǒuzhòng-jiǎoqīng		dizzy	60

	突飞猛进	tūfēi-měngjìn		(of a cause, learning, etc.) advance by leaps and bounds	51
	团结	tuánjié	动	unite	58
	推	tuī	动	push	59
	退役	tuì yì	动	retire	56
	拖	tuō	动	mop	53
W	完全	wánquán	副、形	completely; fully; absolute	50
	玩具	wánjù	名	toy	53
	晚会	wǎnhuì	名	party; gala	52
	万事如意	wànshì-rúyì		realize all one's wishes	64
	网站	wǎngzhàn	名	website	57
	忘	wàng	动	forget	56
	危险	wēixiǎn	形	dangerous	59
	维持	wéichí	动	maintain; keep	50
	尾巴	wěiba	名	tail	58
	未来	wèilái	名	future	56
	胃	wèi	名	stomach	59
	胃口	wèikǒu	名	appetite	60
	温泉	wēnquán	名	hot spring	62
	文学	wénxué	名	literature	57
	稳定	wěndìng	形	stable; steady	51
	污染	wūrǎn	动	contaminate; pollute	58
	无价	wújià	动	priceless	61
	无人不知	wúrén-bùzhī		to a proverb; known to all	55
	无所适从	wúsuǒshìcóng		at a loose end; not know what to do	64
	五洲四海	wǔzhōu-sìhǎi		whole world; all parts of the world	53
	悟	wù	动	understand; comprehend	61
X	吸引	xīyǐn	动	attract	57
	稀	xī	形	watery; thin	60

喜悦	xǐyuè	形	happy; cheerful	53
先生	xiānsheng	名	Mr.	55
显得	xiǎnde	动	look; seem; appear	53
险	xiǎn	形	dangerous	51
限制	xiànzhì	动、名	restrict; restriction	61
陷	xiàn	动	sink into	58
陷入	xiànrù	动	be caught in	52
馅儿	xiànr	名	stuffing	54
相连	xiānglián	动	be tied (to); be bound up (with)	58
相信	xiāngxìn	动	believe	50
享有	xiǎngyǒu	动	enjoy	55
响彻云霄	xiǎngchè- -yúnxiāo		(of sound) very loud and clear	57
响遏行云	xiǎng'è- -xíngyún		(of singing) be so sonorous that it stops the passing clouds	57
想念	xiǎngniàn	动	miss	64
向往	xiàngwǎng	动	yearn for	56
项目	xiàngmù	名	sports event	49
小说	xiǎoshuō	名	fiction; novel	57
笑容	xiàoróng	名	smile	55
写作	xiězuò	动	write	57
泄气	xiè qì	动	lose heart; feel discouraged	51
心甘情愿	xīngān- -qíngyuàn		willingly	64
心灵	xīnlíng	名	heart; soul	55
心酸	xīn suān	形	feel sad	63
新闻	xīnwén	名	news	55
幸运儿	xìngyùn'ér	名	lucky dog	50
凶恶	xiōng'è	形	fierce; ferocious	58

胸怀	xiōnghuái	动、名	have in mind; mind	63
许愿	xǔ yuàn	动	make a wish	53
宣传	xuānchuán	动	publicize	52
悬崖峭壁	xuányá-qiàobì		precipice; cliff	61
旋律	xuánlǜ	名	melody	57
选举	xuǎnjǔ	动	elect	58
穴位	xuéwèi	名	acupuncture point; acupoint	50
学前教育	xuéqián-jiàoyù		preschool education	63
学士	xuéshì	名	bachelor	63
学位	xuéwèi	名	academic degree	63
寻找	xúnzhǎo	动	look for; search	52
Y 严重	yánzhòng	形	serious; critical	59
研究	yánjiū	动	research; study	55
眼泪	yǎnlèi	名	tear	63
演出	yǎnchū	动	perform; show	57
宴会	yànhuì	名	feast; banquet	64
养	yǎng	动	recover; recuperate	60
痒	yǎng	形	itchy	60
腰	yāo	名	waist	50
遥遥领先	yáoyáo- -lǐngxiān		be far ahead; hold a safe lead	49
药材	yàocái	名	medicinal material	61
药农	yàonóng	名	herb farmer; herb collector	61
要不	yàobù	连	otherwise; or else; or	51
也许	yěxǔ	副	maybe	54
野生	yěshēng	形	wild	58
业余	yèyú	形	amateur	52
一辈子	yíbèizi	名	all one's life	63
遗憾	yíhàn	形、名	regretful; regret	49

一般	yìbān	形	general; so-so	56
一方面	yì fāngmiàn		on the one hand	57
一齐	yìqí	副	at the same time; together	53
一言为定	yìyánwéidìng		It's a deal.	63
以	yǐ	介、连	with; by means of	51
以为	yǐwéi	动	think; believe; consider	59
椅子	yǐzi	名	chair	53
议论	yìlùn	动、名	discuss; comment	51
异口同声	yìkǒu- -tóngshēng		with one voice; in unison	61
译本	yìběn	名	translation	55
意识	yìshí	动、名	realize; be aware of; consciousness	58
意味着	yìwèizhe	动	signify; mean	64
因此	yīncǐ	连	therefore; hence	55
音容	yīnróng	名	voice and look (of sb.)	55
饮食	yǐnshí	名	food and drink; diet	52
英雄	yīngxióng	名	hero	49
赢得	yíngdé	动	win; gain	51
硬	yìng	形、副	hard	54
永（远）	yǒng (yuǎn)	副	always; forever	55
勇敢	yǒnggǎn	形	brave	54
用法	yòngfǎ	名	usage	54
优秀	yōuxiù	形	excellent; outstanding	57
幽默	yōumò	形	humorous	57
悠扬	yōuyáng	形	melodious	57
尤其	yóuqí	副	especially; particularly	52
由	yóu	介	(*used for showing how or in what way sth. is done*) by	50
游览	yóulǎn	动	go sightseeing; tour	61

有情有义	yǒuqíng-yǒuyì		having affection and faith	58
有志者事竟成	yǒuzhìzhě shì jìng chéng		Where there's a will, there's a way.	57
幼儿	yòu'ér	名	child	63
幼儿园	yòu'éryuán	名	kindergarten; nursery school	63
愚蠢	yúchǔn	形	stupid; foolish	57
语重心长	yǔzhòng-xīncháng		(say sth.) in all earnestness	52
预备	yùbèi	动	get ready	49
预订	yùdìng	动	book; reserve in advance	61
原理	yuánlǐ	名	principle; theory	50
原谅	yuánliàng	动	forgive	54
原文	yuánwén	名	the original	55
圆梦	yuán mèng	动	make one's dream come true	56
乐队	yuèduì	名	band; orchestra	57
乐团	yuètuán	名	philharmonic society	55
岳	yuè		high mountain	62
云海	yúnhǎi	名	sea of clouds	62
运动会	yùndònghuì	名	sports meeting	49
运动员	yùndòngyuán	名	sportsman or sportswoman	56
运输	yùnshū	动	transport	64
Z 灾难	zāinàn	名	disaster; calamity	58
在座	zàizuò	动	be present (at a meeting, banquet, etc.)	64
赞成	zànchéng	动	approve of; agree with	55
脏	zāng	形	dirty; unclean	53
早日	zǎorì	副、名	soon; at an early date	64
造	zào	动	make	51
增长	zēngzhǎng	动	increase; rise	63
炸	zhá	动	fry	63

粘	zhān	动	stain	54
战略	zhànlüè	名	strategy	64
战士	zhànshì	名	soldier	58
章法	zhāngfǎ	名	methodicalness	51
掌权	zhǎng quán	动	wield power	51
照应	zhàoyìng	动	look after; take care of	61
折合	zhéhé	动	convert into	61
针	zhēn	名	needle	50
针灸	zhēnjiǔ	名	acupuncture	50
珍藏	zhēncáng	动、名	treasure up; rare and valuable articles collected and treasured up	61
诊断	zhěnduàn	动	diagnose	59
争强好胜	zhēngqiáng-hàoshèng		aggressive; pushy	56
整体	zhěngtǐ	名	whole; entirety	51
政府	zhèngfǔ	名	government	56
知识	zhīshi	名	knowledge	52
直	zhí	副、形	continuously; straight	58
值日	zhírì	动	on duty	62
指挥	zhǐhuī	动、名	conduct; conductor	55
至于	zhìyú	动、介	go as far as to; as for; as to	55
制造	zhìzào	动	make	58
制止	zhìzhǐ	动	stop	58
治疗	zhìliáo	动	(by means of medicine, operation, etc.) treat; cure	50
致富	zhìfù	动	become rich; make a fortune	64
智者	zhìzhě		wise man	64
终场	zhōngchǎng	动	end (of a performance or game)	51
终点	zhōngdiǎn	名	finish	49
终生	zhōngshēng	名	all one’s life	63

衷心	zhōngxīn	形	heartfelt	63
重	zhòng	形	important	49
重量	zhòngliàng	名	weight	51
重视	zhòngshì	动	attach importance to	58
周游	zhōuyóu	动	travel round	55
粥	zhōu	名	porridge	60
煮	zhǔ	动	boil	54
住持	zhùchí	名、动	(Buddhist or Taoist) abbot	61
住院	zhù yuàn	动	be hospitalized	59
祝贺	zhùhè	动	congratulate	49
祝愿	zhùyuàn	动	wish	64
著名	zhùmíng	形	famous	51
专栏	zhuānlán	名	special column	55
专门	zhuānmén	副	specially	61
专心致志	zhuānxīn- -zhìzhì		be absorbed (in); absorbedly	55
转交	zhuǎnjiāo	动	pass on to	52
转眼	zhuǎnyǎn	动	in an instant; in a flash	64
壮观	zhuàngguān	形、名	magnificent; grand sight	62
滋润	zīrùn	动	nurture	55
滋味	zīwèi	名	taste; experience; feeling	61
自满	zìmǎn	形	feel complacent; self-satisfied	57
自然	zìrán	名、形、 副	nature; natural; naturally	58
自由	zìyóu	形、名	free; freedom	61
总统	zǒngtǒng	名	president	58
走廊	zǒuláng	名	corridor	52
足球赛	zúqiúsài	名	soccer game	51
组成	zǔchéng	动	form; make up; compose	50

最近	zuìjìn	名	recently	50
尊重	zūnzhòng	动	esteem; respect	55
作家	zuòjiā	名	writer; author	57
作曲家	zuòqǔjiā	名	composer	55
作为	zuòwéi	介	as	55
做法	zuòfǎ	名	way of doing or making sth.	52

专名 Proper Nouns

巴黎	Bālí	Paris	64
曹操	Cáo Cāo	name of a person	51
曹冲	Cáo Chōng	name of a person	51
长江三峡	Cháng Jiāng Sān Xiá	the Three Gorges of the Yangtze River	61
成都	Chéngdū	Chengdu	61
重庆	Chóngqìng	Chongqing	61
村上	Cūnshàng	name of a person	55
大连	Dàlián	Dalian	60
大卫	Dàwèi	name of a person	49
戴维	Dàiwéi	name of a person	50
东方	Dōngfāng	the East	55
东汉	Dōng Hàn	Eastern Han Dynasty	51
法一	Fǎyī	name of a person	61
河野	Héyě	name of a person	52
华清池	Huáqīng Chí	Huaqingchi	62
黄春燕	Huáng Chūnyàn	name of a person	63
黄山	Huáng Shān	Mount Huang	62
可慧	Kěhuì	name of a person	61
丽江	Lìjiāng	Lijiang	62
联合国	Liánhéguó	United Nations	58
美穗	Měisuì	name of a person	52
南山寺	Nánshān Sì	Nanshan Temple	61
秦国	Qín Guó	State of Qin	57
秦青	Qín Qīng	name of a person	57
秦始皇	Qín Shǐhuáng	Qinshihuang, the first emperor of China	62
青木	Qīngmù	name of a person	63